Songs of the Servant

To my mother's memory.
She served the Servant.

Songs of the Servant
Henri Blocher

Inter-Varsity Press

INTER-VARSITY PRESS

Universities and Colleges
Christian Fellowship
39 Bedford Square, London WC1B 3EY
Inter-Varsity Christian Fellowship
Box F, Downers Grove, Illinois 60515

ISBN UK 0 85110 579 3
ISBN USA 0 87784 559 X

Library of Congress Catalog Card No. 75–9068

Quotations from the Bible are from
the Revised Standard Version
(copyrighted 1946 and 1952,
Second Edition 1971, by the
Division of Christian Education,
National Council of the Churches of
Christ in the United States of
America), unless otherwise stated.

Printed in Great Britain by
Richard Clay (The Chaucer Press) Ltd
Bungay, Suffolk

Contents

6124

Preface

The substance of this little book originated as Bible Readings for the seventh General Committee of the International Fellowship of Evangelical Students at Mittersill, Austria, in 1971. Encouragement from some of those who heard the talks has led me to put them into print. I sorely realize how far short my words fall of a full commentary on the great Isaiah's great prophetic poems, but such are the overflowing riches of these inspired passages that I trust the reader will not go away empty, however inadequate the channel.

The written form has kept quite close to what was given orally. Though I cannot claim that it is a scholarly work, it has benefited, I hope, from my study of such books, and should lead many of its readers to commentaries more complete and more profound.

Many thanks are due, and are here offered, to the publishers for their patience and for their correction of a poor Frenchman's English!

Henri Blocher

Approaching the Songs: Jesus and the Servant **1**

But an angel of the Lord said to Philip, 'Rise and go toward the south, to the road that goes down from Jerusalem to Gaza.' This is a desert road. ²⁷And he rose and went. And behold, an Ethiopian, a eunuch, a minister of Candace, queen of the Ethiopians, in charge of all her treasure, had come to Jerusalem to worship ²⁸and was returning; seated in his chariot, he was reading the prophet Isaiah. ²⁹And the Spirit said to Philip, 'Go up and join this chariot.' ³⁰So Philip ran to him, and heard him reading Isaiah the prophet, and asked, 'Do you understand what you are reading?' ³¹And he said, 'How can I, unless some one guides me?' And he invited Philip to come up and sit with him. ³²Now the passage of the scripture which he was reading was this:

> *'As a sheep led to the slaughter*
> *or a lamb before its shearer is dumb,*
> *so he opens not his mouth.*
> *³³In his humiliation justice was denied him.*
> *Who can describe his generation?*
> *For his life is taken up from the earth.'*

³⁴And the eunuch said to Philip, 'About whom, I pray, does the prophet say this, about himself or about some one else?' ³⁵Then Philip opened his mouth, and beginning with this scripture he told him the good news of Jesus. ³⁶And as they went along the road they came to some water, and the eunuch said, 'See, here is water! What is to prevent my being baptized?' ³⁸And he commanded the chariot to stop, and they both went down into the water, Philip and the eunuch, and he baptized him. ³⁹And when they came up out of the water, the Spirit of the Lord caught up Philip; and the eunuch saw him no more, and went on his way rejoicing (Acts 8:26–39).

And they were on the road, going up to Jerusalem, and Jesus was walking ahead of them; and they were amazed, and those who followed were afraid. And taking the twelve again, he began to tell them what was to happen to him, [33] *saying, 'Behold, we are going up to Jerusalem; and the Son of man will be delivered to the chief priests and the scribes, and they will condemn him to death, and deliver him up to the Gentiles,* [34] *and they will mock him, and spit upon him, and scourge him, and kill him; and after three days he will arise.'*

[35] *And James and John, the sons of Zebedee, came forward to him, and said to him, 'Teacher, we want you to do for us whatever we ask of you.'* [36] *And he said to them, 'What do you want me to do for you?'* [37] *And they said to him, 'Grant us to sit, one at your right hand and one at your left, in your glory.'* [38] *But Jesus said to them, 'You do not know what you are asking. Are you able to drink the cup that I drink, or to be baptized with the baptism with which I am baptized?'* [39] *And they said to him, 'We are able.' And Jesus said to them, 'The cup that I drink vou will drink; and with the baptism with which I am baptized, you will be baptized;* [40] *but to sit at my right hand or at my left is not mine to grant, but it is for those for whom it has been prepared.'* [41] *And when the ten heard it, they began to be indignant at James and John.* [42] *And Jesus called them and said to them, 'You know that those who are supposed to rule over the Gentiles lord it over them, and their great men exercise authority over them.* [43] *But it shall not be so among you; but whoever would be great among you must be your servant,* [44] *and whoever would be first among you must be slave of all.* [45] *For the Son of man also came not to be served but to serve, and to give his life as a ransom for many'* (Mk. 10:32–45).

The first disciple from Africa was brought to Christ through Bible exposition. Ethiopia's chancellor of the exchequer had already been attracted to Judaism; through Philip's exposition he came to understand both the ancient scripture which he was reading, and who Jesus was.

And what was this scripture? Since Luke quotes it at length in his account in Acts, it is easy to recognize: it was the well-known passage in Isaiah 52:13–53:12 which depicts a mysterious, suffering and triumphant Servant of the Lord. This is usually called 'the fourth Servant Song', for there are at least three other passages in the second part of the book of Isaiah (chapters 40 to 55) which have to be taken together with it. The first of these Songs starts with a formula like that which introduces the fourth Song: 'Behold, my servant' (Is. 42:1;

cf. 52:13). The second and third Songs show marked affinities in language and content with the first and the fourth. They surely refer to the same figure, and it would not be incorrect to say that the wider 'text' on which Philip based his expository sermon was the whole group of Servant Songs.

Philip's use of them (or the Holy Spirit's use of them through Philip) is no isolated case. The story is more than an account of a heartwarming incident: it is also a significant illustration of the way in which the early church looked upon these prophetic passages, and of the central place which they held in Christian thought and witness at the time when the flame of the Spirit was beginning to spread.

The Servant in the preaching of the apostles

Take the evidence we have about the Jerusalem church, shortly after Pentecost. In the space of two chapters, Jesus is called the Servant four times (Acts 3:13, 26; 4:27, 30). In fact, this title is so prominent that some scholars have said that christology—the doctrine of the person of Christ—was then primarily paidology (from *pais*, the Greek word for servant). Jesus was first proclaimed as the Servant. Peter offers a clear summary of the teaching of the fourth Song in his bold address to the crowd (Acts 3:13–15):

> The God of Abraham and of Isaac and of Jacob, the God of our fathers, glorified his servant Jesus, whom you delivered up and denied in the presence of Pilate, when he had decided to release him. But you denied the Holy and Righteous One, and asked for a murderer to be granted to you, and killed the Author of life, whom God raised from the dead.

Still dazed after the tremendous crisis they had just undergone at Pentecost, the disciples laid hold of the Servant prophecies as the one sure word which had foretold the facts of Jesus' life, death and resurrection; and which revealed with unsurpassed clarity their meaning.

When Christ's witnesses turned to the Gentiles, the *title* 'Servant' lost its earlier primacy; at any rate, we do not find it in the records in the later chapters of Acts. The titles 'Christ', 'Lord', 'Son of God', would be used instead. Because these titles already had certain uses in the non-Jewish world, they were more intelligible to people unfamiliar with the Old Testament than the term 'Servant'. The title 'Servant', more than any other, required a knowledge of the Old Testament background in order to be understood. The writings of the apostles, however, show that the Servant *theme* remained very important, and that the Servant Songs were decisive in shaping the Christians' understanding of Jesus.

The importance of the theme may be seen in Peter's first Letter, as well as in his Jerusalem speech. The apostle leans heavily on the last Servant Song. For the benefit of his readers, most of whom were Gentiles, he gives an interpretative rendering of several verses, applying them to the Christian life.

But if when you do right and suffer for it you take it patiently, you have God's approval. For to this you have been called, because Christ also suffered for you, leaving you an example, that you should follow in his steps. He committed no sin; no guile was found in his lips. When he was reviled, he did not revile in return; when he suffered, he did not threaten; but he trusted to him who judges justly. He himself bore our sins in his body on the tree, that we might die to sin and live to righteousness. By his wounds you have been healed. For you were straying like sheep, but have now returned to the Shepherd and Guardian of your souls (1 Pet. 2:20–25).

Paul, too—the apostle 'untimely born'—is at one with his Jerusalem colleagues in his dependence upon the Songs in Isaiah. As early as his visit to Pisidian Antioch during the course of his first missionary journey, he refers to the second Song as being fulfilled in the mission (Acts 13:46, 47; *cf.* Is. 49:6). Writing to the Roman church, he quotes Isaiah's complaint: 'Who has believed what he has heard from us?' (Rom. 10:16; *cf.* Is. 53:1). From this he adduces the principle that 'faith comes from what is heard', which in turn provides a powerful motive for preaching Christ. Again, he draws from the same Servant Song his principle of concentrating on unevangelized fields (Rom. 15:20, 21; *cf.* Is. 52:15). In all these instances,

Paul is vindicating his missionary activity—a burning issue for him personally.

We hear a clear echo of the Servant Songs in two other passages which mark key developments in Paul's theology, Paul's grasp of the gospel ('my gospel', as he could call it). The first of these sets out the great parallel and the great contrast between the two Adams: between the first Adam, and Christ, who is the new Adam (Rom. 5:12–21). In this passage Paul contrasts that fatal rebellion, the disobedience of our first father, with Christ's obedient submission to the Father's will. In Christ, men, though sinners, may now be 'made righteous'. This justification, or acquittal, of 'many', is the fruit of the one act of obedience of the one man Jesus Christ. Now this is precisely the message of the last Servant Song, even using the same words: the righteous Servant will 'make many to be accounted righteous' (Is. 53:11). As we shall see, the word 'many' should be taken as an almost technical expression in the Songs. Was Paul meditating on the Servant Songs when he was led to his emphasis on justification; free justification based on Christ's obedient sacrifice?

Paul again stresses Christ's obedience (and obedience is the mark of any servant) in the famous hymn in Philippians 2:5–11, which he either wrote himself or adapted for use in his Letter. Unlike Adam, who coveted equality with God, Jesus Christ came to serve. He humbled himself even to death; he poured out his own life, as it were, in service to others. Because he accepted that way of suffering, he has been lifted up, exalted to supreme heights. One might almost be reading another version of the last Servant Song, the two hymns are so much alike.

Again and again in the New Testament we come across quotations from, or allusions to, the Servant Songs. Matthew's Gospel twice points to Servant passages which were fulfilled in Christ's ministry. The first is quoted in connection with his miracles of healing, which are a fruit of his sacrifice (8:17; cf. Is. 53:4). The second quotation illustrates Christ's rejection of the noisy publicity with which people wanted to surround him (12:15–21; cf. Is. 42:1–4). The Letter to the Hebrews, too, underlines the prophetic statement, 'He bore the sins of many' (9:28; cf. Is. 53:12). And John, like Paul, recalls

Isaiah's prediction of Israel's hardness of heart (Jn. 12:37, 38; *cf.* Is. 53:1; Rom. 10:16).

John also records the wonderful phrase with which John the Baptist greeted Jesus: 'Behold, the Lamb of God' (Jn. 1:29). This title, 'the Lamb of God', probably refers us back to several Old Testament 'types' of Christ; it is synthetic in character. But it can hardly be separated from the Servant Songs, which compare the Servant to a submissive sheep led to the slaughter. The Lamb of God will take away (or 'bear'; both meanings are intended) the sin of the world; the Servant will carry the sins of the guilty, the sins of the many. There may even be a pun contained in the word 'Lamb', although this suggestion lacks proof: scholars have pointed out that the one Aramaic word, *talya'*, can mean both 'lamb' and 'servant'.

This shower of Bible references should be enough to make our point: in all quarters and strata of New Testament Christianity, the Servant passages are found to be the clue to the work of Jesus.

And now the question arises, 'How has this come about? Why are the writers so unanimous?' One could answer, 'Well, just because of the facts of the case!' Isaiah's description fits the real Jesus so precisely that one could not but interpret the one in terms of the other.

When a blind man's eyes are opened, however, he often needs to be taught to see, even to see the obvious. The Gospels make it clear that Peter and the others were not innovating when they applied the Servant prophecies to Jesus. Jesus himself had done it first. Peter just followed his Master: he had been taught to see.

The Servant in the self-understanding of Jesus

Jesus was the first to see that the Servant was none other than himself. It was with reference to the function and character of the Servant that he interpreted his very Messiahship. Jesus' whole Christology—the way he, as the Messiah, viewed his own person and mission—has been summarized in this way: Jesus repudiated the common, worldly expectation of the Messiah; his view was, instead, a balanced blending of the Messianic concept with two other figures described in the pages of the

Old Testament. One of these figures was the Son of man whom Daniel saw in a vision (Dn. 7:13, 14): he was to be a heavenly being, coming into the presence of the Ancient of Days, the eternal God himself; and to him were to be given everlasting dominion, glory and kingly power—this was not to be corruptible power like that of an earthly king.

The other figure was Isaiah's suffering Servant. Jesus understood that the Christ and the Son of man and the Servant were one person, himself. Most of his fellow Jews expected a merely human Messiah, another David, a hero who would deliver Israel from her political bondage to the Romans. Jesus saw that the true Messiah was not only Son of David, as the kingly Messiah was expected to be, but also David's Lord (Mt. 22:41-45 and parallels). The way of triumph for this Messiah, the way by which his everlasting kingdom would be set up, was not military prowess; he would defeat his enemies, as Isaiah foresaw, by surrendering himself to an atoning death.

World-famous scholars, even outside evangelical circles, have championed this insight. Joachim Jeremias and Oscar Cullmann, to name two examples, have highlighted the importance of the Servant Songs for Jesus. Recently, however, some scholars have tried to deny it altogether. A British theologian, Miss Morna D. Hooker, has argued that the fifty-third chapter of Isaiah had practically no influence on our Lord.[1]

But if we take the Gospels at face value—and there is no reason why we should not—we see that for Jesus, his ministry was bound up with the role of the Servant from the very beginning. What was the word from heaven which was given to our Lord when he was baptized in the Jordan? The Father proclaimed: 'Thou art my Son, the Beloved, with thee I am well pleased' (Lk. 3:22, margin). Now, this can be recognized as a combination of two Old Testament verses. 'Thou art my Son' comes from the second Psalm: Jesus is addressed as the supreme anointed King of the Davidic line, the Messiah. The second part of the heavenly address is very similar to some words at the beginning of the first Servant Song: 'My chosen, in whom my

[1] In *Jesus and the Servant* (SPCK, 1959). For a masterly refutation of these negative views, see R. T. France, 'The Servant of the Lord in the Teaching of Jesus', *Tyndale Bulletin*, 19, 1968, pp. 26–52.

soul delights' (Is. 42 : 1); Jesus is assigned that strange mission
which is outlined in Isaiah's prophetic poems. And immediately after his baptism, Jesus was pushed into the wilderness by the Spirit (Mark uses a very strong verb in 1 : 12) to be
tempted there by the devil. What was the heart of Jesus'
temptation? The devil tried to entice him with the current
view of Messiahship: Jesus replied, in effect, that he would
stick to the Servant pattern which the Father had revealed to
him.

More than once in the course of his ministry, Jesus alluded to
the Servant Songs. Once, James and John, the sons of Zebedee,
asked for the privilege of sitting on either side of Jesus when
he was in his glory. They, perhaps, did not understand Jesus'
answer: 'You do not know what you are asking. Are you able
to drink the cup that I drink, or to be baptized with the baptism with which I am baptized?' We, however, know that
Jesus was thinking ahead to the cup of God's wrath which he
would have to drink, to the baptism of death which he would
have to undergo. The Servant prophecies were in his mind. He
added significantly that the way to glory in his kingdom is just
the reverse of what it is in the world: for earthly rulers, the
exercise of authority means trampling down others, but the
first among the followers of Jesus must be *servants* of all. And
then came the decisive statement: 'The Son of man also came
not to be served but to serve, and to give his life as a ransom for
many.' This is the last Servant Song in a nutshell, with, again,
that typical word 'many'. Jesus used it again a little later, when
he dramatically announced his imminent death; he had given
his disciples the wine to drink: 'This is my blood of the covenant, which is poured out for many' (Mk. 14:24).

During that same last supper, Jesus found yet another op-
portunity of recalling a Servant passage. Luke has preserved
for us a recollection of an actual quotation by Jesus. Our Lord
had warned his disciples about the darkness which was soon to
fall upon them. He had used figurative language which they
failed to understand: 'Let him who has no sword sell his mantle
and buy one.' Then he spoke as plainly as possible: 'This
scripture must be fulfilled in me; "And he was reckoned with
transgressors"; for what is written about me has its fulfilment'
(Lk. 22:37; *cf.* Is. 53:12).

The way in which Jesus uses this quotation is most interesting. It reveals why Jesus so often used that word 'must'. Repeatedly, from the time when Peter confessed him as the Christ at Caesarea Philippi (Mt. 16:13–20 and parallels), Jesus tells his dull-sighted disciples that the Son of man *must* be delivered into the hands of men, and suffer, and be put to death, and then rise again. Why did Jesus say '*must*'? Some passages make the answer clear: Jesus must go this way because Scripture so directs him. But which scripture, more precisely? Usually we are not told. Only here, in Luke 22, is it revealed: it was in the Servant Songs that Jesus found the way.

To be sure, other passages in the Old Testament may be listed as prophecies of the cross; yet there is none with the clarity and precision of the Songs. Apart from an indefinite number of 'types', several Psalms (*e.g.* Pss. 22, 69) poignantly told in advance of the sufferings of the Messiah; but they must be thought of as *indirectly* Messianic (for some statements are applicable only to the Old Testament king or righteous sufferer). There are hints in Daniel's revelations that the Messiah will have to die: the principle of trial before triumph appears here (Dn. 7:21, 25; 12:7); a mysterious oracle foretells an 'anointed one' (or Messiah) cut off (Dn. 9:26); but without the help of Isaiah we should not understand it. Only in Zechariah is it almost as clear as in Isaiah: remember the rejected shepherd; the Lord's companion against whom the sword shall awake; the pierced one who will be bewailed as Josiah was; a fountain opened for sin and uncleanness (Zc. 11; 13:7; 12:10; 13:1). Zechariah's prophecies, however, are not easily understood by everybody. Zechariah himself recalls the Isaianic Songs in his vision of the universal and absolute Day of Atonement, on which the Lord 'will remove the guilt of this land in a single day': in this vision the coming one is given a double title, 'my servant, the Branch' (Zc. 3:8). This title unites the suffering Servant of the Songs and the Son of David promised by Jeremiah (23:5).

So we are led back to the Servant Songs. In them our Saviour found the blueprint of his mission. From them Jesus learned that he would have to suffer for us; that he would die for us, as though he were a criminal, under the weight of our sins. How holy the ground we tread when studying the Songs!

How unspeakably moving it is to imagine Jesus meditating upon those passages, and knowing that this was the Father's will and way for him; that this Servant was none other than himself.

It is hard for us to conceive how Jesus was able to learn, since as the Son the total knowledge which God possessed was his from all eternity. And yet this truth is revealed in the Bible: although he was the Son, he had to learn. Perhaps he decided, as he laid aside his glory, not to make use of his divine omniscience. It is a difficult subject. In any case, we must beware of detracting from the reality of Christ's humanity: he came as one of us. As we rightly confess Christ's absolute deity, we may easily forget that he was flesh and blood, a man under the discipline of learning. He had to learn. He did not read the Scriptures just in order to apply them to others, or just as a concession to his contemporaries. As a man he needed the Scriptures. To him as to ourselves—to him especially—they were the Father's voice, the Father's light, food given to him by his Father. Particularly so were these words in Isaiah, so precise, so clear; so terribly precise and clear.

Our approach

We do not know better than our Lord. There can be nothing more important for our own understanding of the Servant Songs than Jesus' understanding of them. So the first axiom of our approach should be the certainty that the Servant is Jesus. In these poems, composed centuries before his earthly life, the evangel of our Lord is being proclaimed from afar. Yet we should not simply search for New Testament verses to fit all the predictions in Isaiah. This can be done with profit, and the margin of a study Bible offers all that is needed. But such a search may bring with it a tendency to level down the diversity of Scripture, to dry up the life which may be seen in its historical development. Their common inspiration does not mean that we should take all the words of the Bible as if they were said by the same man at the same time.

Here even investigations by scholars of generally doubtful theological opinions may help us to grasp what God has revealed. Interpreters so sadly misdirected as to fail to see Jesus

at the focal point of the Servant Songs may none the less un-
cover data useful in our search for understanding: they may
help us to recognize more accurately the historical context of
the Songs, and to appreciate their place within the organic
development of prophecy.

Those who disagree with the New Testament's Christic
interpretation of the Songs fall into two main categories. Some
say that the Servant, in the mind of the writer, is *an individual
but not the Messiah*: others say that the Servant figure is a
literary device, *a symbol representing Israel*. There are also
syntheses of the 'Messianic' and 'collective' views, and there
are modern, 'fluid' interpretations which suit contemporary
dialectical thought (the Servant is Israel and he is not; he is
Christ and he is not); we shall leave these aside.

Among identifications suggested by scholars in the first
category (those who hold the 'individual', non-Messianic view),
we can cite the following: Moses; Job (the primary referent of
the Songs according to Pope Adrian I in the time of Charle-
magne); a king such as Josiah or Hezekiah; Zerubbabel; or a
prophet, especially Jeremiah or the author himself. (Such
scholars hold that the author was a 'deutero- (second) Isaiah',
an unknown prophet living in Babylon 150 years later than
Isaiah.) The very multitude of names shows the weakness of
this type of interpretation. A noted German scholar, Ernst
Sellin, successively propounded four different solutions in the
course of his academic career. You may search in every corner
of the Old Testament: no man of God, however great, has the
required stature to be the Servant. Yet scholars in this first category have rightly grasped an important point: the concrete-
ness of the picture demands that the prophecies refer to a real
person. Surely, also, the Servant bears resemblances to several
Old Testament figures (in the immediate context, Cyrus, king
of Persia, is addressed in Isaiah 45 in ways reminiscent of the
Servant Songs). God's Spirit did not work in a vacuum; he
used concepts already in the prophet's mind. The lesson for us
is that we should take into account whatever partial models
may have been used in the description of the Servant.

In the second category, too, there is variety. The Servant,
say scholars in this group, is Israel. This is variously taken to
mean empirical, historical Israel; or the ideal Israel; or a part

of Israel, the faithful remnant. These 'collective' interpretations are based on an obvious and important fact: in the section
of Isaiah's book where the Songs are found, similar language is
used for the Servant and for Israel (see, *e.g.*, 41:8 ff.). Such
striking phrases as 'my servant', 'I have formed you', 'I have
called you (from the womb)', 'I have chosen you', 'I uphold
you', are common to the Servant Songs and the Israel passages.
And yet there are contrasts which are even more striking than
the similarities. Israel is a blind and deaf servant: the Servant
is the perfect listener, and he will be as a light. Israel is a
rebellious, wayward servant, and suffers deserved punishment:
the Servant is the sinless one, whose death is for the people. The
Servant will have a mission to Israel, and will restore the
remnant. How could the one be taken for the other? Such a
confusion could result only from a gross misreading of the text.
When the whole section (chapters 40–55) is read at one sitting,
the Servant Songs stand out most impressively. We cannot let
ourselves be carried away with 'collective' interpretations.
Yet these interpretations rightly highlight one biblical fact:
similar language is used throughout the section. The lesson
for us is that we should be sensitive to the relationship between the Songs and the neighbouring passages which speak of
Israel.

Accordingly, the second axiom of our approach will be the
fact that the Songs occur in a definite literary context. The
Songs are not to be considered as isolated units.

This will help us to solve a small preliminary problem: that
of the precise limits of some of the Songs. Scholars agree as to
their beginnings, but opinions vary concerning concluding
verses. The Songs lead so smoothly into the passages which
follow them that it is hard to tell exactly where they end. We
shall adopt Professor Bruce's idea of 'connecting links'; bridges
between the Songs and their contexts.[2] Sometimes it is thought
that the Songs fell meteor-like into the text: other people take
the opposite view, that the Songs are just ordinary parts of the
development and should not receive special consideration as a
group. Professor Bruce's idea enables us to avoid this unfortunate dilemma. Our working hypothesis is this: the prophet

[2] F. F. Bruce, *This is That: the New Testament Development of Some Old
Testament Themes* (Paternoster, 1968), p. 84.

composed the Songs separately from the rest of the second part of his book, though he intended them to be included. When he inserted them, he added connecting verses, where we find a continuation of the thought of the Songs as well as strong echoes of the context.

We shall take the limits of the Songs to be as follows: the references in brackets indicate the connecting links.

First Song	Isaiah 42:1–9 (5–9)
Second Song	Isaiah 49:1–13 (7–13)
Third Song	Isaiah 50:4–11 (10,11)
Fourth Song	Isaiah 52:13—53:12

To these four passages we would add a brief but weighty Servant oracle, Isaiah 51:16, and we would mention chapter 61, a prophecy closely related to the Servant Songs.

Our study will attempt to be Christic and contextual. And, of course, it will not despise the practical benefits of such a study. Although the application is for each person to make in his own heart and life, the third axiom of our approach will be the need to recognize the pattern laid down in the Songs for our own service. May God help us not to forget that Jesus himself recalled the last Servant Song when teaching his disciples the way to glory, which was also to be his glory way; and Peter quoted from it with the comment that 'you should follow in his steps' (Mk. 10:41–45; 1 Pet. 2:21).

Behold my servant, whom I uphold,
my chosen, in whom my soul delights;
I have put my Spirit upon him,
he will bring forth justice to the nations.
²*He will not cry or lift up his voice,*
or make it heard in the street;
³*a bruised reed he will not break,*
and a dimly burning wick he will not quench;
he will faithfully bring forth justice.
⁴*He will not fail or be discouraged*
till he has established justice in the earth;
and the coastlands wait for his law.

⁵*Thus says God, the Lord,*
who created the heavens and stretched them out,
who spread forth the earth and what comes from it,
who gives breath to the people upon it
and spirit to those who walk in it:
⁶*'I am the Lord, I have called you in righteousness,*
I have taken you by the hand and kept you;
I have given you as a covenant to the people,
a light to the nations,
⁷   *to open the eyes that are blind,*
to bring out the prisoners from the dungeon,
from the prison those who sit in darkness.
⁸*I am the Lord, that is my name;*
my glory I give to no other,
nor my praise to graven images.
⁹*Behold, the former things have come to pass,*
and new things I now declare;
before they spring forth
I tell you of them' (Is. 42: 1–9).

The Spirit of the Lord God is upon me,
because the Lord has anointed me
to bring good tidings to the afflicted;
he has sent me to bind up the brokenhearted,
to proclaim liberty to the captives,
and the opening of the prison to those who are bound;
² *to proclaim the year of the Lord's favour,*
and the day of vengeance of our God;
to comfort all who mourn;
³   *to grant to those who mourn in Zion—*
to give them a garland instead of ashes,
the oil of gladness instead of mourning,
the mantle of praise instead of a faint spirit;
that they may be called oaks of righteousness,
the planting of the Lord, that he may be glorified.
⁴ *They shall build up the ancient ruins,*
they shall raise up the former devastations;
they shall repair the ruined cities,
the devastations of many generations (Is. 61:1–4).

The later prophecies of Isaiah, beginning at chapter 40, are
usually known as 'the Book of Consolation' because they open
with these words: 'Comfort, comfort my people, says your
God.' As the author of the apocryphal book of Ecclesiasticus
summed it up: 'By the spirit of might he (Isaiah) saw the last
things, and comforted those who mourned in Zion' (48:24).

Why were God's people mourning? Why were they to be
comforted now? Isaiah's vision carries him across time and
space into the situation of exile he himself had foretold to
King Hezekiah (39:5–7). The children of Israel and Judah
have settled as captives in Babylon. They have lost everything:
Jerusalem is a heap of ruins, and the hill on which the temple
stood is now uncultivated and overgrown with vegetation. The
people have long been deprived of king or prince, of sacrifice
and sacred pillar. They have lost heart. The Lord, they com-
plain, has forsaken them. Perhaps his power is confined to the
land of Judea, and he can no longer help them now that they
are exiled in the plains of Babylon. Perhaps, some of them
probably wonder, the Lord has been defeated by the gods of
Babylon; for it was commonly thought that the god of the

victorious nation was mightier than the gods of nations which
had been conquered. Dry bones—these will be the symbol
which Ezekiel will use in his prophecy about these discouraged
captives (Mi. 3:12; Ho. 3:4; Is. 40:27; Ezk. 37:1–14).

To this people, dwelling in dark despair, dwelling in the
shadow of national death, Isaiah has a message of comfort to
bring. The Lord is the only one, the only true God. He alone
is master of the universe; he alone is the ruler of all history. His
plans are not made in accordance with the expectations of
men; men cannot fathom his thoughts. The downfall of Judah
and the sufferings endured in captivity have been the outwork-
ings of his righteous judgment. But now the Lord is about to
reveal again the riches of his steadfast love. New things are soon
to break upon the nation. The Lord will soon stretch out his
powerful arm, as he did in the exodus of former times. In order
to show that the God of Israel is the God of all the earth, that
he deals with all men as a potter deals with clay, moulding
them for his own purposes, he will use a pagan conqueror to
carry out his plan. Cyrus, the Persian king, will subdue Babylon
and the nations. But his astounding victories will be the Lord's
doing. Cyrus will be Israel's deliverer from this new house of
bondage, Babylon. When Israel hears of his success, the people
must rejoice: the Lord has not withdrawn his electing grace; he
still stands with them, and fights on their side. When this
victorious warrior is first mentioned, his identity is not dis-
closed—he is simply called 'one from the east'—but later even
his name, Cyrus, is given (41:1–4; 44:28; 45:1).

But is Cyrus the only deliverer who is to come? These prophecies which describe the new exodus sing a redemption much
more wonderful than the return from exile that Cyrus permit-
ted upon his take-over in Babylon. They sing a redemption
much more wonderful even than the first exodus, for all its
miracles. It will change the wilderness into a garden of the
Lord. It is heralded as a new creation. It is bound up with an
outpouring of God's Spirit like renewing rain upon the people
(43:16–21; 48:6, 7; 44:3). All this is much more than Cyrus
can do. Obviously the role of Cyrus is only introductory, and
his campaigns are only a prelude to what the Lord is going to
do. That is why, after Cyrus has been introduced, another
deliverer steps in. Unlike Cyrus, he remains anonymous; the

Lord calls him simply 'my servant'. The Lord himself introduces him: this introduction we call the first Servant Song.

This Servant of the Lord will perform wonders: he will
open the eyes that are blind, and bring out the prisoners from
the dungeon where they sit in darkness. We cannot doubt that
he is to be the deliverer who brings about the new exodus. His
work goes far beyond that of Cyrus. But it will also be a different sort of work: he will be a deliverer of an altogether
different kind. What will he be like? This we shall now try to
understand.

The man of God's choosing

In the opening verses of the first Song, the emphasis falls
upon the relationship of the Servant to God's will. As the Servant, he has surrendered himself fully to be used as an instrument in the fulfilment of God's purposes. But the main
thrust of the first verse is not so much that he will be obedient
as that he is the object of God's choice. Three expressions are
used to convey this idea. God says that the Servant is the one
'whom I uphold'. The word means 'hold fast'. God will have
the firmest grip on his Servant. He will be entirely on the Servant's side, and close to him.

Then the Servant is called 'my chosen', my elect one. In the
baptism greeting from heaven to Jesus, the Gospel writers
have taken over the Hebrew word used here and have translated it into a Greek one meaning 'beloved' (Mt. 3:13–17 and
parallels). This rendering reminds us of the close relationship
between will or choice and love; between *electio* and *dilectio*.
All too often we think of love as a matter of feeling—and so it
is—but primarily it is a matter of choice and will. A close
friend, a husband, a wife, is not just a person to whom we feel
emotionally drawn but a person with whom we have deliberately chosen to develop a relationship, a person whom we set
apart in our minds and attitudes from the other people we meet
day by day. This element of decision and choice distinguishes
loving from merely liking or being acquainted with a person.
So, the Servant is not chosen simply to carry out a specific task,
but is set apart as his Lord's beloved one.

And then the Lord says that the Servant is the one 'in whom

my soul delights'. 'My soul' is often another way of saying 'I' or 'myself'. But the word is often used when the person's inner desires and longings are playing a part in or being affected by the activity in question. So when we read that the Lord's soul delights in the Servant, we may understand it to mean that the Servant will be the man who fulfils and satisfies all the Lord's desires for humanity. Can we sense this joy, the joy of the Father who has found the man in whom he may delight? So many of his servants have failed him, but now at last there is one man in whom he can fully delight. Do we adequately realize that God *delights* in his chosen ones who carry out his purposes? If we really love God, the desire that he should be able to delight in us will be a terrific driving force in our lives.

Jesus, then, is this chosen one, God's elect one. Theologically and practically (and we cannot separate theology from practice) this truth is one on which we ought to meditate much more often than we do. We tend to overlook it, because regrettably we tend to think of election only as God's act of choosing individual sinners to be saved. Now election, in the New Testament, certainly is a choosing of individuals for salvation, but we sadly impoverish the biblical doctrine of election if we forget that Christ is the first chosen one. Augustine and Calvin did not forget this fact, and they put a lot of emphasis on the thought that Christ is 'the mirror of election'. By this they meant that to see Christ as the elect one helps us to discern that election depends solely upon God. Christ's humanity by itself is nothing; it exists only as something which the Son of God took upon himself, and its unique privileges antedate all the meritorious works of the man Jesus. But in Christ we also see that election cannot be divorced from obedience; in him God is able to delight because he does God's will. In this mirror, too, we can see that the salvation which is provided for us cannot be separated from the means of its provision, which was the work of Christ as the head of the body of the elect. We see ourselves chosen *in him*, as Paul puts it: he is our head, and our election in him binds us together in one body (see Eph. 1).

Election entails the gift of the Spirit. The Lord says of the Servant: 'I have put my Spirit upon him.' This again shows the Servant's utter dependence upon God in all that he will have to do, and it shows the closeness of their relationship.

The Servant will be the permanent bearer of God's presence, power and wisdom. Indeed, these three terms—God's presence, God's power and God's wisdom—describe what the gift of the Spirit implies. At the same time, the Servant is singled out to play a decisive role in the salvation which will be manifest in the last days, for the Old Testament promises that it is then that the Spirit will be given. The Servant, as bearer of the Spirit, is the one who works salvation in the last days. And of course the New Testament recognizes that the last days began with the coming of Christ (*e.g.* Heb. 1:1, 2; 1 Pet. 1:20).

Earlier in the book of Isaiah (11:1, 2), there is another figure upon whom the Spirit of the Lord will rest. The Spirit of the Lord—the Spirit of wisdom, of might, of the fear of the Lord—will rest upon the Scion of David, the promised Messiah; for the title 'Messiah' was ordinarily used of that new and perfect Solomon, who, since Nathan's oracle (2 Sa. 7) was expected to appear. Are we to draw the conclusion that the Servant and the coming King of peace are one and the same person? In fulfilment at least, it was so. Again we remember the scene at the river Jordan: the Holy Spirit came to rest upon him whom the Father greeted as Servant and as Messiah. If the prophet did discern clearly that the Servant and the Messianic King would be the same person, he was not led in the first Song to assign him a king's mission. Instead, the Servant appears as a preacher or one of the wise: as a *teacher*.

The teacher of truth

As we think of the Servant as a teacher, our mind's eye catches a glimpse of Jesus, the travelling rabbi. It was as a rabbi that Jesus chose to fulfil his ministry. But let us return to the prophetic Song.

The Servant is to 'bring forth justice' (verse 1). The word rendered in most modern versions by 'justice' is a very common one in the Old Testament, but a difficult one to translate. It is the word *mišpat*, which means first 'judgment' and then 'custom', 'law'. In the Mosaic law it is frequently used as a synonym of 'commandment', 'statute'. What God has judged to be right he has taught or given as a precept to his people. Most commentators think that in the prophecies of Isaiah it has a wide meaning and becomes practically synonymous with true religion. According to the etymology of the word, however, the emphasis is probably not on man's obligations but on God's decision, God's judgment. What God has decided, that the Servant will interpret to God's people. This will be his mission. Verse 3 in the Song makes the meaning more precise: 'He will *faithfully* bring forth justice.' A better rendering than 'faithfully' is 'for truth' or 'according to truth'. This phrase strikes a major note in the Song. It shows what the Servant's outlook is as he carries out his work.

In verse 4 there is another word which is worth studying. The word is a well-known one, *tôrâ*, which means 'instruction', and which Judaism has consistently used for the whole body of instruction which Moses delivered to the people. 'The coastlands (the islands and Mediterranean coastal areas of Palestine) wait for his law'; for the Servant's *tôrâ*.

Two typical pentateuchal words, then, are used in this Song, and both are given a remarkable significance. Moses had brought forth *mišpat*, and prophets since his time had called upon the nation to practise and return to the judgments which God had given to him. Moses had been the mediator of God's *tôrâ* to Israel. But now Isaiah is prophesying about a Servant whose ministry will be like that of Moses!

The manner in which the Servant teaches deserves notice. 'He will not cry or lift up his voice, or make it heard in the street' (verse 2). Matthew's Gospel (12:15–21) quotes this statement to illustrate Jesus' humble refusal of publicity. The Servant's manner contrasts with that of certain frenzied, ecstatic prophets who used to practise in Old Testament times. Not even the thunderings of an Elijah will characterize him. He will teach truth with a quiet unobtrusiveness. However, the primary contrast is with Cyrus. The character of Cyrus is used as a foil for the Servant's altogether different character. No doubt Cyrus will make a lot of noise in the world. He will come with the glamour and flourish of worldly success. Not so the Servant. Cyrus will deliver Israel by scattering kings by sword and bow; coasts and islands will tremble with terror because of his fame (41:2, 5). Not so the Servant. He will deliver men from blindness by means of calm teaching and patient persuasion; coasts and islands will look to him in expectancy, waiting for his *tôrâ*. Of course this suggests that it will be another kind of exile from which the Servant will deliver his people.

The fundamental point of difference between Cyrus and the Servant is that the Servant is concerned about truth. Cyrus is primarily concerned not with truth but with military triumph. The Servant has a passion for truth. What is right by divine definition, what is 'according to truth', must be established on earth in men's hearts and relationships.

How important it is that we should remember this! C. S. Lewis, in *God in the Dock*,[1] has a passage relevant to this thought. Lewis says that people want to be shown whether Christianity is good. This is not the question, he says. The real question is, Is it *true*? People try to avoid this question. In the prevailing subjective and utilitarian climate of thought we are in danger of losing that overriding concern for absolute truth which the Lord loves. In its place, we may become over-concerned with the efficiency of our evangelism and devote all our energies to winning the maximum number of converts in the shortest possible time, regardless of whether they have truly repented or not. Or we may emphasize intensity of religious experience, as though Christianity were a thrill or a trip. Again, we may trim the gospel up (or water it down) in an attempt to make it conform to modern thought forms. But if we yield to any of these temptations, we are being motivated by concerns wholly different from that concern for truth which motivated the Servant.

Now, revelation is not given in a vacuum. We may legitimately ask how it came about that Isaiah was led to describe the Servant in these terms rather than in any others. He contrasts him with Cyrus. But did he find in his Old Testament world some figures from which he could draw positive analogies to help him in his portrayal of the Lord's Servant? The answer to this question is Yes.

One's thoughts turn first to the prophets, since, like the Servant but on a smaller scale, it was their task to make known God's truth, God's judgment. Whenever Israel's national and religious life was in ruins, the prophets stood as the only servants with whom the Lord could be at all pleased.

[1] Edited by Walter Hooper (Eerdmans, 1970).

In the course of Israel's history the kings, with some exceptions, had gone from bad to worse. The priests had for the most part forsaken their duties. They had even polluted the worship of the Lord with idolatry. Only a few faithful prophets in the course of the nation's history had remained as God's true witnesses. Was it because kingship and priesthood were established institutions, the offices of king and priest being handed down from father to son, whereas the prophets depended immediately upon God for their commission and the ability to fulfil it? In view of the disappointing record of the kingly and the priestly lines, perhaps Isaiah was led by the Spirit to portray the future Saviour as the perfect Prophet.

But he was not to be entirely like the other prophets: he would not be on a level with them. We find in verse 6 a very important statement: 'I have given you as a covenant to the people.' This could not be said of any kind of prophet. When one says 'covenant' one thinks of Sinai, and of Moses who was also called the servant of the Lord (Ex. 14:31). Moses was the great teacher of truth who had brought forth God's *mišpat* and God's *tôrâ*, the instructions to Israel which formed the foundation of her national life and her religion. As we read Isaiah's first Servant Song, the name of Moses flashes in the background. The decisive point is that Moses himself had promised that God would raise up a prophet *like himself*, Moses (Dt. 18:15). Moses had left the horizon of the future open; he had done no more than foretell the coming of a new Moses. Is it not obvious? Isaiah is building upon previous revelation. The Servant whom he is describing can be no other than the new Moses whom we find already promised in the book of Deuteronomy.

This new Moses will not be just another Moses. The concluding verse of the Song celebrates the newness of what God will soon cause to spring forth. This newness seems to be closely connected with the Servant's ministry. The former things, the promises and foreshadowings in the Mosaic dispensation, have come to pass. For the old dispensation, the exile was really the beginning of the end (*cf.* Heb. 8:13). New things which then were just beginning to germinate are now coming to fruition. The Song intimates that there will even be a new display of God's creative power. Why does the prophet recall the creation of heaven and earth if not to suggest that God is about to create new heavens and a new earth, a new order and a whole new humanity, as it were, as the Servant fulfils his mission? The complete and outward fulfilment of this hope is yet to come; but spiritually, as Paul says, 'if any one is in Christ, he is a new creation; the old has passed away, behold, the new has come' (2 Cor. 5 : 17). The study of the other Servant Songs and oracles will further reveal the Servant's complete superiority over Moses. In the first prophecy, two aspects of this superiority are brought to light.

The mediator of grace to all

The most obvious difference between Moses and the Servant is that the scope of the Servant's mission is much wider than the scope of the mission assigned to Moses. Both Moses and the Servant were appointed 'as a covenant to the people'. But whereas Moses' mission was to the people of Israel alone, the Servant is to be 'a light to the nations'. The Servant 'will bring forth justice to the nations' (the Gentiles), and his *tôrâ* will reach to the uttermost parts of the earth.

The apostle Paul appealed to this promise when he had to vindicate his mission to the Gentiles (Acts 13:46–48). He saw his work—which was really Christ's work continued through his apostle—as the fulfilment of the Servant's task. Through Paul, Jesus the Servant was bringing to the nations the light of salvation and the freedom of the new exodus (*cf.* Lk. 2:25–32, especially verse 32). Earlier, the aged Simeon, in the prophetic prayer which we know as the *Nunc dimittis*, had greeted the infant Jesus with these words from the first Servant Song. Our Lord himself claimed this universal ministry. He made it clear that when he was lifted up from the earth, he would draw all men to himself. The Servant was to be a universal Moses. Jesus fulfilled this function.

The second difference is more subtle. It appears in a literal translation of verse 3 and the first part of verse 4:

> A bruised reed he will not break,
> A dimly burning wick he will not quench;
> But he will bring forth justice according to truth;
> He will not burn dimly or be bruised.

In the Hebrew the same pair of verbs—meaning 'to bruise' and 'to burn dimly'—is used in both verses. What is the significance of this? Israel, her national identity threatened by exile, was a bruised reed and a dimly burning wick. These images are reflections, too, of our own condition without God, beaten and blown by forces of evil with which we cannot cope. But he, the Servant, will not be bruised. His light will never be extinguished. Because the Servant will be obedient to the end, even to the point of death for sins not his own, his light will never grow dim. He will endure incomprehensible agonies in God's service and will not be beaten down by them. He will not yield to the pressures to which we constantly, sinfully, yield: he will not. He will patiently go on without fainting.

As the victor over temptation, the Servant would have every right to break the bruised reed and to quench the dimly burning wick. Israel, and we ourselves, have failed and disobeyed. Justice demands that we should be finally broken, that our faint light should be quenched. But *he will not*. This is the amazing message of the prophecy. He will not quench what light there is. He will not condemn sinful Israel, or our sinful selves. Moses, the meekest of all men in his time (Nu. 12:3), is nothing to be compared with the new Moses, the Servant of the Lord. There is something ineffably tender in the Servant's compassion; he will stoop over us, he will not quench us, he will spend his own life to heal the bruised reed, to revive the fainting wick. There is only one word for this—*grace*.

The new Moses will be the covenant prophet of a new covenant of grace for both Jews and Gentiles. 'The law was given through Moses;' wrote John the evangelist, 'grace and truth came through Jesus Christ' (Jn. 1:17). Because grace, in order truly to be grace, cannot be restricted by human and national barriers, the Servant's gracious mission, too, will be universal in this sense.

John, proclaiming that grace had come through Christ, also testifies that *we* have received from his fullness grace upon grace. The sixty-first chapter of Isaiah is a prophecy which has many parallels with the first Servant Song: in both there are the themes of the prophetic role, the deliverance of the captives and the anointing of the Spirit. In this chapter the proclaimer of good news is not by himself, but in the company of glorious Zion. Mourners turned rebuilders, anointed with the oil of gladness and clothed in the mantle of praise, will surround him as a plantation of righteousness. What a promise, what grace, to us bruised reeds and fainting wicks!

The second Song: Head of redemption

> *Listen to me, O coastlands,*
>> *and hearken, you peoples from afar.*
> *The Lord called me from the womb,*
>> *from the body of my mother he named my name.*
> 2 *He made my mouth like a sharp sword,*
>> *in the shadow of his hand he hid me;*
> *he made me a polished arrow,*
>> *in his quiver he hid me away.*
> 3 *And he said to me, 'You are my servant,*
>> *Israel, in whom I will be glorified.'*
> 4 *But I said, 'I have laboured in vain,*
>> *I have spent my strength for nothing and vanity;*
> *yet surely my right is with the Lord,*
>> *and my recompense with my God.'*

> 5 *And now the Lord says,*
>> *who formed me from the womb to be his servant,*
> *to bring Jacob back to him,*
>> *and that Israel might be gathered to him,*
> *for I am honoured in the eyes of the Lord,*
>> *and my God has become my strength—*
> 6 *he says:*
> *'It is too light a thing that you should be my servant*
>> *to raise up the tribes of Jacob*
>> *and to restore the preserved of Israel;*
> *I will give you as a light to the nations,*
>> *that my salvation may reach to the end of the earth.'*

> 7 *Thus says the Lord,*
>> *the Redeemer of Israel and his Holy One,*
> *to one deeply despised, abhorred by the nations,*

the servant of rulers:
'Kings shall see and arise;
princes, and they shall prostrate themselves;
because of the Lord, who is faithful,
the Holy One of Israel, who has chosen you.'

[8] *Thus says the Lord:*
'In a time of favour I have answered you,
in a day of salvation I have helped you;
I have kept you and given you
as a covenant to the people,
to establish the land,
to apportion the desolate heritages;
[9] *saying to the prisoners, "Come forth,"*
to those who are in darkness, "Appear."
They shall feed along the ways,
on all bare heights shall be their pasture;
[10] *they shall not hunger or thirst,*
neither scorching wind nor sun shall smite them,
for he who has pity on them will lead them,
and by springs of water will guide them.
[11] *And I will make all my mountains a way,*
and my highways shall be raised up.
[12] *Lo, these shall come from afar,*
and lo, these from the north and from the west,
and these from the land of Syene.'
[13] *Sing for joy, O heavens, and exult, O earth;*
break forth, O mountains, into singing!
For the Lord has comforted his people,
and will have compassion on his afflicted (Is. 49:1–13).

In the second Servant Song, as in the first, there is a twofold structure. Again, the second part acts as a connecting link with what follows, emphasizing the theme of deliverance; God is the speaker and he is addressing the Servant.

The first part of the poem, however, is in the first person singular. The Servant himself is speaking. This is exceptional. Apart from the third Servant Song, and the kindred prophecy of Isaiah 61, this kind of I-discourse is found nowhere else in the entire book of Isaiah. When the prophet tells us about events in his own life (for instance, when he recounts his call to the prophetic office in chapter 6, or his dramatic encounter with King Ahaz in chapter 7) the style, mood and situation are altogether different. The kind of I-discourse which we have in the second Song is found only when God is the speaker. God— and the Servant. Is this striking detail a hint of what Peter was to unfold centuries later (in 1 Pet. 1:10–12); that the Spirit who revealed God's plan to the prophets was not only the Spirit of God, but the Spirit of Christ? If Isaiah is inspired by the divine Spirit of the Servant, then the Servant may speak in the first person when his future sufferings and the glory which is to follow are revealed. At any rate, this form of discourse makes the presentation of the Servant more intimate. We penetrate into his situation, as it were. We are able to see more clearly the Servant's relationship, first to God and then to the Gentiles. Our study will follow this order.

The Servant and God

The Servant's dependence on God is stressed once more. The idea which we find in the opening verses of the Song is similar to the idea present in the beginning of the first Song: God upholds the man of his own choosing. But there is a slight difference. In theological terms this difference could be expressed in the following way: in the first Song we are told about the Servant's *election*; in the second Song we are told about his *predestination*.

The Servant has been called 'from the womb'. This idea is typical of the records of the calling of individuals to a specific and unusual ministry. It is found in the calling of Jeremiah and of Paul (Je. 1:4, 5; Gal. 1:15). The Servant has been set apart and given his name and his role in the fulfilment of the divine purposes right from the beginning of his human existence. This phrase 'from the womb' surely shows that God's grace precedes and antedates any possible human merit. Paul, writing about God's choice of Jacob and his passing over Esau, emphasizes that the choice was made before either had done right or wrong. God's election is sovereign, independent of human works, and therefore absolutely primary. It is contem-

poraneous with the very commencement of our being. What
we later become due to the predestination of God is not added
to our being; it is our being itself.

There is great comfort in this thought. I once read a book
which led me to picture life as a stage. In life we all play a
variety of parts, we relate in different ways to different people.
It cannot be otherwise. I am referring not to hypocrisy, which
is deceitful and self-distorting, but to the fact that we each have
a number of faces and that we always remain at some distance
behind them. This distance is good; it is essential to person-
hood. Without it there would be no freedom to know others
and to be known by them, and thus to enter into personal
relationships. Our personalities are revealed only by means of
the 'face' we present to those to whom we choose to make
ourselves known, and the 'face' varies according to the relationship we bear to each of those persons. There is no insincerity
here: it is simply that when I relate to my parents I play the
part not of a husband or wife but of a son or daughter; when I
relate to my lecturers I play the part not of a son or daughter
but of a student. But if we think much about this fact, anxiety
creeps in. All these faces, all these roles—among them all, who
am *I*? Among all these names I bear, which is mine? Here lies
the difficulty: if I say that my being is identical with them—if
I say, 'I am a student and I am a son and I am this, that and
the other . . .', my being is exploded. There is no longer any
unity. If I claim to be other than a collection of faces and
names, where am *I*? If who I am is not just a student plus a
son plus all the other faces, what is the relationship between all
these faces and myself? Am I just an abstract point of conver-
gence? If so, I am nothing. If I say that behind all my faces I
have an innermost being which is not a role or face, then what
is that? It too sinks into nothingness. And so I lose myself again.

There is only one way out of this dilemma. If I have a name,
a role, which is truly and radically 'I', and which unites all the
other roles, then I am safe. If my innermost being is that role
and name which God has given me from my mother's womb,
then there can be unity. The role, the name, which God pre-
destinates is the foundation and justification of whatever
partial names and roles we may have. I should no longer fear
that my various faces in life are going to absorb my being. No,

my being is well founded and unified in the role which God has given me. This role, moreover, has a context in the whole plan of God.

The role of the Servant is that he is to be God's instrument. We can even call him God's weapon, for he is compared to a sharp sword and a polished arrow. These military images suggest that the Servant's ministry is not only one of work but one of war and struggle. Isaiah has not previously suggested this.

The Servant says: 'He has made my mouth like a sharp sword.' The sword is a favourite image in Scripture for the word of God (cf. Eph. 6:17). The word of God is a two-edged sword able to penetrate the deepest recesses of our being, and able to discern the thoughts and intentions of the heart (Heb. 4:12). Again we are led to see the Servant primarily as a prophet, as *the* Prophet who brings and even is God's Word.

But the strange thing is that in this Song the sword and the arrow are hidden from sight. The arrow is in the quiver, and the sword is concealed in the shadow of God's hand. What is the significance of this concealment? It is a fitting picture of the Servant's intimate communion with the Lord, a communion whose fullest richness is unseen by others. It corresponds to the quiet and lowly manner of the Servant in his ministry, of which we saw a description in the first Song. But, more significant, it indicates that there will be a specific hour for the fulfilment of the Servant's mission. He is already being used by the Lord, but his real work is still hidden from sight until God draws the sword and shoots the arrow. There will be a specific moment when God will use his Servant to defeat the enemy and thus to be glorified through his Servant.

In this struggle, the Lord will answer the Servant's prayers and come to his aid. 'In a time of favour I have answered you, in a day of salvation I have helped you' (verse 8). In prayer to the Father, Jesus said: 'Thou hearest me always' (Jn. 11:42). The Lord will vindicate his Servant, who confesses: 'Surely my right is with the Lord' (verse 4). God will reward him and glorify him. Here is the first suggestion of a theme which is very prominent in John's Gospel: God and Christ glorify each other. The Son glorifies the Father, and the

Father glorifies the Son (*e.g.* 17:5). In this Song, the Servant will glorify the Lord, and the Lord will glorify the Servant (verses 3, 4, 7).

The Servant and Israel

The Lord addresses the Servant by a well-known name: 'You are my servant, *Israel*, in whom I will be glorified' (verse 3). What is the relationship of the Servant to Israel? Some scholars want to delete the name Israel here. The Jerusalem Bible, for instance, puts it in brackets and notes that it is probably a gloss.

But we lack sufficient evidence from the old manuscripts and versions to allow such an emendation. We had better accept the surprising fact that the Servant is here addressed by the name Israel. Does this mean that he is no more than a literary personification of Israel? This is not a necessary conclusion. The name Israel may be used in a polemical sense: in the phrase 'Israel, in whom I will be glorified', there are overtones of criticism of the nation. Was God glorified in his collective servant Israel? That was Israel's trouble. The nation had received as its mission the charge to glorify the Lord, to be his obedient servant, but it had failed. The nation had been a blind messenger, a deaf servant of the Lord (42:18 ff.). The one in whom the Lord will be glorified is the one who deserves the name of Israel. When God says to the Servant, 'You are Israel,' he is indirectly rebuking the nation.

In addition, the Song makes it clear that the Servant is to be distinguished from the people. For it is his mission to bring Jacob back to the Lord, to gather Israel to him, to raise up the tribes of Jacob and to restore the Israelites who had been preserved. How then can the Servant be a personification of Israel? The 'preserved of Israel' are the faithful remnant, so the Servant cannot be identified even with them. He cannot be a mere literary personification of the people.

The image of the exodus is obviously being used in this Song. In all these chapters the Servant, as we have seen, is the deliverer for whom the people are waiting. This Song proclaims that the Servant will be the leader of a return; he will be the leader of a new, universal exodus. The exodus images can easily be recognized: '. . . saying to the prisoners, "Come forth," to those who are in darkness, "Appear." They shall feed along the ways, . . . they shall not hunger or thirst' (verses 9 f.). In the first exodus, God delivered his people and provided them with manna to eat and water to drink in the wilderness. The new redemption will extend to all the corners of the earth: 'Lo, these shall come from afar, and lo, these from the north and from the west, and these from the land of Syene' (verse 12; Syene, or Sinim, is almost certainly to be identified with the Aswan area in upper Egypt). All will arise to discover light and liberty, pastures and bubbling streams.

Now it is quite clear from what we have already seen of the Servant that the physical exile, the Babylonian captivity, and the physical return from it, are used as 'types' of the state from which the Servant will deliver his people. Cyrus was a deliverer on a physical level, but the Servant will be a deliverer of another kind, on a different level. Isaiah is not the first to have given the exodus theme this typical, spiritual significance. One very interesting passage was written earlier, in the eighth century BC; it is found at the end of the book of Micah (7:15). God is speaking of the new deliverance which he will perform for his people. 'As in the days when you came out of the land of Egypt I will show them marvellous things.' This is a most definite promise of the new exodus. What kind of exodus is it to be? 'Who is a God like thee' Micah asks (7:18), echoing the famous triumph song of Moses after the crossing of the Red Sea (Ex. 15), 'pardoning iniquity and passing over transgression for the remnant of his inheritance?' The deliverance has to do with sin. Later, the same passage makes this even clearer: 'Thou wilt cast all our sins into the depths of the sea' (Mi. 7:19). In the first exodus it was the Egyptians and their chariots that were cast into the Red Sea: now God is going to deal in an equally final and devastating way with our sins. Isaiah was building on the foundation laid by the previous prophets in his use of the exodus theme.

So the Servant cannot be confused with Israel; he is the new Moses of the new exodus. Why then is he called Israel? There are two biblical concepts which can help us to understand the strange relationship of the Servant to the people, his bearing their name while being distinct from them. The first is that of headship—covenantal headship. Many scholars today think that what they call 'corporate personality' is the key to Hebrew mentality. It is much better to recognize that this is not just a structure of Hebrew mentality, but the teaching of Scripture. Men are not merely individuals, added to one another yet independent of each other. No man is an island. We really belong together. We actually share in the same being. God has created us in communities which must not be thought of as accidental groupings of self-contained units. Communities and the bonds that bind us are essential dimensions of human life. A community has a real unity which is expressed in its head. This applies especially to covenant communities. God's covenant with Adam and thus with the whole human race; God's covenant with Abraham and with Moses and thus with Israel; a man's marriage covenant with a woman, too: all exhibit the same structure. They institute headed communities. The head sums up or represents the whole, yet it cannot be mistaken for the body, not even in a kind of vague, fluid dialectic between the two. It is the head, not the body. And yet, at the same time, the body is nothing without the head, and the head truly expresses the body. Now the Servant seems to be the head of Israel, the head of that community which he is to redeem and restore.

The second concept is what is known as Delitzsch's pyramid. Franz Delitzsch was not an ancient Egyptian pharaoh but a German evangelical scholar in the nineteenth century. He showed from the Bible that as the history of salvation proceeds, the scope of God's redemptive dealings with man seems to grow narrower and narrower. God starts, as it were, with the whole human race, first at the time of Adam, and then again after the Flood. Then one line of the human race is chosen: God makes his covenant with Abraham and his descendants. But he does not make it with all Abraham's descendants: only Isaac and his line are chosen—Isaac, not Ishmael. Even among Isaac's children, only one—Jacob, not Esau—is chosen. And then, getting narrower, the prophets make it clear that not all those who descend from Israel (Jacob) are truly Israel. Only a remnant will inherit the promise. But where is this remnant when we look for it? When God looks for a man to intervene and establish justice in the land he finds none (Is. 59:16;

Ezk. 22:30). Ultimately only one person remains after the sifting process, only one is truly Israel, in whom God is glorified. And he said so. He said quite clearly, 'I am the true Israel.' He used the Old Testament's most common symbol for Israel; the vine: 'I am the true vine' (Jn. 15:1 ff.; *cf.* Ps. 80:8–16; Is. 5:1–7; Je. 2:21; 6:9; Ho. 10:1; see also Mt. 21:33–43 and parallels). In him the pyramid reaches its apex.

The lines, however, do not stop there. Starting from Christ, there is a symmetrical broadening. In him, the true Israel, the true vine, are the branches which feed on his life and are purified by him. Those who find salvation in him inherit the promise which belongs to the true remnant. To them also, in a secondary sense, the name Israel truly belongs (Rom. 9:6–8; Gal. 3:6–9; 6:15, 16; Phil. 3:3). All the Gentiles who have faith in Christ are incorporated into this community. So this new Israel, the Israel of God, is a new humanity, spreading over the whole earth. As the second Song puts it, the Servant is to be 'a light to the nations, that my salvation may reach to the end of the earth'. What perfect geometry in God's plan!

The Servant and the Gentiles

The Gentiles are the first group to be addressed by the Servant, right at the beginning of the second Song. 'Listen to me, O coastlands, and hearken, you peoples from afar' (verse 1). The Lord's language is even more striking. He says to the Servant: 'It is too light a thing that you should be my servant to raise up the tribes of Jacob . . .'—it is not enough that the Servant's ministry should be to his own people alone—'I will give you as a light to the nations' (the Gentiles: verse 6). We see again how much greater is the new Moses than the old. The light which the Servant will bring will be not only that of true doctrine but also the light of salvation.

This theme agrees with the many missionary passages in the book of Isaiah. The prophet has already introduced the basis for a theology of mission. The promise that the heathen will share in the Lord's salvation occurs throughout the book. In the very chapter which contains the second Servant Song, there is a reference to Zion's unexpected children whom she finds with her on the day of her redemption (49:20, 21):

The children born in the time of your bereavement
    will yet say in your ears:
'The place is too narrow for me;
    make room for me to dwell in.'
Then will you say in your heart:
    'Who has born me these?
I was bereaved and barren.'

In chapter 54 and later chapters we find mention of children who have been given suddenly and miraculously to Zion. Paul, quoting from the fifty-fourth chapter, explained to the Galatians how these oracles ought to be understood (Gal. 4:26–28, quoting Is. 54:1). The children are the Gentiles who have been engrafted, who are by grace given the right to belong to the true Israel of God. More Christians have been Israelites by grace alone than by grace and race. When we see how early God's missionary purpose was revealed, we feel ashamed that the Christian church was so slow in recognizing it, and that we ourselves are often so apathetic to God's command.

Among the Gentiles, there will even be kings who will bow down before the Servant. Worldwide glory will be given to him. And of course this has been literally fulfilled in the history of the Christian church. There have been kings who have bowed down before the Servant-Christ. In his *Memorial* from St Helena, Napoleon found moving words to acknowledge the superior glory of Jesus during the time of recollection and meditation which God granted to him after such a roaring and destructive career.

> Everything in Christ astonishes me. His spirit overawes me, his will confounds me. Between him and whomever else in the world, there is no possible term of comparison. . . . The nearer I approach, the more carefully I examine, everything is above me—everything remains grand, of a grandeur which overpowers.

Ultimately, however, the promise to the Servant means that *all* honour will be his. Whatever glory and honour the nations possess will be gathered into the Servant's Jerusalem (Rev. 21:26). Scripture teaches that every good fruit of human work, every fruit of 'common grace', will be saved and treasured up in the kingdom of God: it will all contribute to the universal praise of the Servant's glory.

But before this triumph, the Servant must be unusually humbled (verse 7). He will be 'deeply despised'. This phrase literally means 'despised of soul'. He will be 'abhorred by the nation' (the noun is singular, though the RSV makes it plural), and 'the servant of rulers', or, as the NEB has it, 'the slave of tyrants'. In the last two Songs we shall see more of this strange path to glory. Here in the second Song, even before we are told that the Servant will be despised, there is a hint that he will meet hostile situations. 'I have laboured in vain,' he says in verse 4, 'I have spent my strength for nothing and vanity.' We are not to think that these words express discouragement. The Servant has not yielded to the pressures put upon him: he will not faint, he will not be bruised. But he was truly *tempted*: discouragement was a possibility for him, but by looking to God in faith he has overcome it.

Is it not encouraging for us to know that he could be tempted to be discouraged? Again we see him as one of us, yet as the one who does not faint and fail where we faint and fail. 'Because he has suffered and been tempted, he is able to help those who are tempted' (Heb. 2:18).

However disappointing our results, however frightening the threats, however hostile the circumstances, we do not lose heart. Following in the Servant's footsteps, we go in faith, we look to God, we see the invisible; our cause is with God, our recompense is in his hands.

The third Song and the oracle: **4**
The Lord's representative

The Lord God has given me
  the tongue of those who are taught,
that I may know how to sustain with a word
  him that is weary.
Morning by morning he wakens,
  he wakens my ear
  to hear as those who are taught.
⁵ *The Lord God has opened my ear,*
  and I was not rebellious,
  I turned not backward.
⁶ *I gave my back to the smiters,*
  and my cheeks to those who pulled out the beard;
I hid not my face
  from shame and spitting.

⁷ *For the Lord God helps me;*
  therefore I have not been confounded;
therefore I have set my face like a flint,
  and I know that I shall not be put to shame;
⁸   *he who vindicates me is near.*
Who will contend with me?
  Let us stand up together.
Who is my adversary?
  Let him come near to me.
⁹ *Behold, the Lord God helps me;*
  who will declare me guilty?
Behold, all of them will wear out like a garment;
  the moth will eat them up.

¹⁰ *Who among you fears the Lord*
  and obeys the voice of his servant,

who walks in darkness
and has no light,
yet trusts in the name of the Lord
and relies upon his God?
11 *Behold, all you who kindle a fire,*
who set brands alight,
Walk by the light of your fire,
and by the brands which you have kindled!
This shall you have from my hand:
you shall lie down in torment (Is. 50:4–11).

And I have put my words in your mouth,
and hid you in the shadow of my hand,
stretching out the heavens
and laying the foundations of the earth,
and saying to Zion, 'You are my people' (Is. 51:16).

The two passages to be taken together in this chapter contrast with each other. Whereas the third Servant Song reads as the most autobiographical of the Songs—the Servant appearing there as a faithful disciple surrounded by human enemies—the Servant oracle in chapter 51 assigns him a cosmic function.

Yet there are two ideas relating to the Servant which can remove the apparent disparity between the two passages. In both the third Song and the oracle we meet the thought that man's ultimate destiny is bound up with the Servant. In both, too, the Servant appears as God's unique representative, whom God vindicates. The concluding comment of the third Song reveals the fate of those who oppose the Servant; they shall walk into their own fire and shall lie down in torment. Everlasting punishment is a recurring theme in the later prophecies of Isaiah—the solemn final note of the book is one example—and we may assume that the third Song is speaking of eternal destiny. The decisive point is this: the fate which each person is going to meet is the outcome of his attitude to the Servant. This is why the Lord asks: 'Who among you fears the Lord, and obeys the voice of his Servant?' As for the oracle in chapter 51, it addresses the Servant as the agent of God's new, eternal creation. Here again, ultimate realities depend on the Servant's fulfilment of his ministry. We shall take the passages in turn.

The Servant as the perfect disciple

In the first two Songs the Servant was introduced as the authoritative teacher. In the third Song, which is another 'I-discourse', he speaks of himself as a disciple. The Servant's relationship to his people is that of a teacher of truth: his relationship to God is that of the perfect learner. In the third Song the Servant utters the following words:

> The Lord God has given me
>   the tongue of those who are taught, . . .
> Morning by morning he wakens,
>   he wakens my ear
>   to hear as those who are taught.

'Of those who are taught.' The same Hebrew word is used twice: it comes from the verb for 'to learn', and means both 'a learned man' and 'a learner', rather like our word 'scholar'. From the context it seems that the latter meaning is intended here. The Servant, though he teaches, is primarily portrayed as a disciple. In these words the Servant expresses his perfect teachability, his continual fellowship with God. He does not perform his daily task in the strength and wisdom of his own original genius. He starts each day with meditation and prayer, in the quietest moments of the day: 'Morning by morning he wakens, he wakens my ear.' That is the right time to hear. He listens to God before he speaks with others, and then when he speaks it is as a disciple, repeating and applying the Master's words.

Very few people today are content to be disciples in this sense. All over the world, in highly technological societies as well as in developing countries, there is a great hunger for more and more education. But almost everywhere the call is for education understood as discovery and creative originality. Students are encouraged to produce their own theories and not to adopt uncritically those of their lecturers. We are not used to accepting 'as gospel' what we are taught. It is difficult for us to assume the biblical attitude of discipleship, which so conflicts with man's natural tendency to self-affirmation.

There is another passage in the Old Testament with a similar

emphasis on teachability and the same image of the open ear.
The fortieth Psalm, verses 6 to 8, reads:

> Sacrifice and offering thou dost not desire;
>   but thou hast given me an open ear.
> Burnt offering and sin offering
>   thou hast not required.
> Then I said, 'Lo, I come;
>   in the roll of the book it is written of me;
> I delight to do thy will, O my God;
>   thy law is within my heart.'

The Letter to the Hebrews quotes these words as being in the
mouth of our Lord when he entered the world for our salvation
(10:5-7).

Perfect teachability! Surely it became flesh in Jesus! Jesus,
while stressing his authority as the Master (see, *e.g.*, Jn. 13 : 13),
was nevertheless an example of teachability to his disciples. He
could even say: 'I do nothing on my own authority but speak
thus as the Father taught me' (Jn. 8:28). He did not claim
creative originality: he did assume the position of a disciple.
And one morning he heard his Father's voice teaching him
in the very passage from which we are learning now.

Then the serenity of the early part of the Song is broken.
The Servant's teachability seemingly leads him down a
strange path (verses 5, 6):

> The Lord God has opened my ear,
>   and I was not rebellious,
>   I turned not backward.
> I gave my back to the smiters,
>   and my cheeks to those who pulled out the beard;
> I hid not my face
>   from shame and spitting.

What is happening? This is literally what our Lord had to
undergo. Because we immediately see the obvious fulfilment of
this prophecy in the suffering of Christ, we may easily forget
the wider reference: suffering and persecution are a general
law for God's servants in the world. More often than not our

willingness to be taught by God means the acceptance of shame and pain. The Old Testament prophets knew that law from experience: 'O Jerusalem, Jerusalem, killing the prophets and stoning those who are sent to you!' (Mt. 23:37). And the Master, who for our sakes made himself the perfect disciple of the Father, accepting suffering, reminded us that no Christian disciple is qualified to apply for exemption from any of his courses of spiritual instruction: 'A disciple is not above his teacher, but every one when he is fully taught will be like his teacher' (Lk. 6:40; *cf.* Mt. 10:24 f.; Jn. 13 and 15).

The Servant's teachability is not weakness or mere passivity or inertness. It is the fullness of strength and courage. Courage is a virtue which is not often seen to be a *Christian* virtue, as it should be. How moving is the brief statement in the Song: 'I have set my face like a flint' (verse 7). In the New Testament we find the same image in just one word, a word which describes Jesus' attitude as he faced death. Luke tells us how Jesus turned towards Jerusalem knowing what cup he would have to drink there. He tells us that Jesus 'set his face' to go to Jerusalem (9:51). Literally translated, the word is 'made solid', 'hardened'. He set his face like a flint, he made it solid; he did not allow it to be weakened by his own emotions, his own human fear of suffering. What courage the Servant—Jesus—had!

Courage, however, must not be confused with stoic resignation, that hardening of the emotions in feigned self-sufficiency. This is an artificial indifference to suffering. Stoic endurance is made of pride and secret despair. The Servant is courageous in hope; it is a courage rooted in faith in God. 'The Lord God helps me' (verse 7). His faith will not be disappointed. The Servant stands, assured that God will vindicate him, clear him of all unjust charges. 'He who vindicates me is near' (verse 8).

This idea of the vindication of the Servant is important: we find it in the New Testament too. Paul, in his first Letter to Timothy, is thought to quote a fragment of an early Christian song (3:16). Its words describe the 'mystery of our religion', its 'open secret': Christ was 'manifested in the flesh' and 'vindicated in the Spirit'. This refers to Christ's resurrection, since he was raised from the dead in the Spirit of holiness (Rom.

1:4). His resurrection, and the sending of the Holy Spirit which was its consequence, were God's vindication of Christ. By them God demonstrated that Christ was indeed his Servant, willing to hear and to do God's will. He had not been a blasphemer as the Jews had thought. This was his acquittal, 'acquittal by resurrection'. If, therefore, we undermine the historical reality of Christ's resurrection, we are casting a doubt upon the Servant's vindication by his Father, the righteous Judge.

The Song invites us to imagine a trial situation. The Servant and his enemies are engaged in a lawsuit; they stand before the judgment seat, they contend at the bar. The vocabulary used here is almost technical forensic language. It is worth studying, because it points to a main feature in the biblical picture of man. Today we have a distaste for juridical thinking; our logic and thought-forms make it difficult for us to work with. As a result, we do not like to think in terms of judgment or condemnation, or that the idea of judgment enters into religion. Contrary to this, the Bible shows man as being accountable to God the Judge. Man cannot live like a beast which acts by instinct and impulse. He has to give an account of his behaviour; he is bound to do the right or to bear his guilt if he does wrong. He is born within a covenant, which is of course a legal bond. He cannot avoid this, even if he tries to reject the idea of a distinction between right and wrong. He cannot help making moral judgments himself, or feeling himself to be accountable for his own actions. He cannot help judging others. Modern anarchists exemplify this; there is a total contradiction on this point in their philosophy. They deny all moral criteria but they cannot help condemning others. Also, as Paul reminds us, man cannot help judging himself (Rom. 2:15). There is a judgment seat within each one of us, and it testifies to us that we are not beings of chance. We are men before God, the righteous Judge. Of course man, though he cannot help making these judgments, still suppresses the truth and perverts what fragments of it he still knows. He does partly blind himself, but he cannot totally lose sight of the standards of justice of which he is aware by reason of his having been made in the image of God. Only when the problem of guilt is dealt with before God, the righteous Judge and

Lord, is reconciliation possible. This is the biblical view. If we lose our awareness that guilt towards God is the centre of our problem, we start drifting away from the biblical message.

In a trial, the judge has to make clear-cut decisions. Since the Servant does nothing of himself, the Lord is entirely on his side. There is no distinction, then, between fearing the Lord and obeying the Servant's commands. 'Who among you fears the Lord and obeys the voice of his Servant?' the third Song asks (verse 10). The RSV and the NEB translate this as a question; the Jerusalem Bible translates it as an exhortation: 'Let anyone who fears Yahweh among you listen to the voice of his servant!' But whichever rendering we prefer, we have to recognize the basic equivalence of the fear of the Lord and obedience to the Servant's commands. The Servant is to be acknowledged as God's representative on earth.

It follows that the enemies of the Servant are enemies of God. Their fate can only be hopeless. This is said in very colourful language in the Song (verses 9, 11):

> Behold, all of them will wear out like a garment,
>   the moth will eat them up. . . .
> This shall you have from my hand:
>   you shall lie down in torment.

Significantly, the wicked, the Servant's opponents, are to burn in their own fire. The beginning of verse 11 is difficult to translate, but the NEB probably does it best:

> But you who kindle a fire and set fire-brands alight,
> go, walk into your own fire
> and among the fire-brands you have set ablaze.

The Servant's accusers will burn in their own fire. Are we to understand hell—the biting, gnawing fire of remorse—as self-accusation?

The Song implies that to fear the Lord and obey his Servant is to trust in the Lord even while walking in darkness. We are to trust. The Servant says in verses 8 and 9:

> Who will contend with me?
>> Let us stand up together.
> Who is my adversary?
>> Let him come near to me.
> Behold, the Lord God helps me;
>> who will declare me guilty?

It is striking to see that these confident words are echoed by Paul, not as Christ's declaration of assurance, but as that of Christ's people (Rom. 8:31–34). We who are in Christ stand in the same position as the Servant. We can say with full confidence that no accusation can reach us. There is no longer any condemnation for us to fear, for God, the righteous Judge, counts us as righteous. He vindicates us, he justifies us. Our destiny and that of the Servant are the same.

The Servant as co-creator

The Servant oracle, as we have called it, has suffered much at the hands of translators. Many versions, including the RSV, the NEB and the Jerusalem Bible, deviate from the original and totally obscure the reference to the Servant. A literal translation would run like this:

> And I have put my words in your mouth, and I have covered you in the shadow of my hand, to plant heavens and to found earth and to say to Zion, 'You my people.'

Grammatically, the subject of the infinitives 'to plant', 'to found' and 'to say' could be God or it could be the Servant. The Lord may be saying either 'that *I* may plant heavens' or 'that *you* may plant heavens'. Since the putting of God's words in the mouth of the person addressed most naturally implies that it is the person addressed who is to speak to Zion, the second possibility is to be preferred. The oracle is a promise, the past tense being a typical 'prophetic perfect'. The recipient of this promise will speak to Zion and therefore he will also be the one who will plant heavens and found earth. Even if we accept the other, less probable, possibility, he would still be associated in an intimate way with the creation of heaven and earth.

Who can this person be? What figure can be found in the book of Isaiah who could be a candidate for this exalted role? We have a clue in the oracle itself. It is a perfectly clear mark of identification: 'I have covered you in the shadow of my hand.' This is familiar. It is one of the images used in the second Servant Song (49:2). There can be no doubt: the person whom the Lord is addressing in the oracle must be the Servant. Many scholars have seen this, showing greater acumen than some translators. The Danish scholar Aage Bentzen would take the whole passage from verse 9 to verse 16 of chapter 51 as a fourth Servant Song. Without going so far, we can speak of a Servant prophecy which shows that the Servant theme has vital ties with its context, the Book of Consolation.

What is the immediate context of the oracle? God, in this chapter, is unfolding the magnificence of the work he will soon perform. The deserts will be changed into a new garden of Eden (verse 3):

> For the Lord will comfort Zion:
>   he will comfort all her waste places,
> and will make her wilderness like Eden,
>   her desert like the garden of the Lord.

This is already suggesting that God's victory will be a kind of new creation; the reference to Eden turns our minds back to God's first creation. As we read on, the corollary of this truth appears: the old heavens and the old earth, together with all rebellious men, will wear into tatters like wool eaten by moths; the same image which we found in the third Servant Song (verses 6–8; *cf.* 50:9).

The prophet again takes up his favourite theme of the new exodus (verses 9 ff.), but he amplifies it and gives it more force. Egypt is there, but is now symbolized, as in several other passages, by Rahab, the great sea-monster or dragon of contemporary mythology (30:7; Ps. 87:4). The Sea of Reeds is there, called 'the great deep'. This is not poetic hyperbole; it is revelation. The new exodus will be much more than a duplicate of the first. It will be cosmic renewal, new creation. Heaven and earth shall pass away, but the salvation of the Lord shall remain for ever.

The new exodus is so radical that it amounts to re-creation. The Servant oracle plainly says that God, the Master of the universe, will bring to pass a new creation as Israel is accepted back into God's favour and family. Long before, Hosea, also a prophet of the new exodus (*cf.* 2 : 14 f.), had been commanded by God to name one of his sons Lo-Ammi, which means 'Not my people', as a symbolic warning to Israel of the Lord's temporary rejection of the nation in judgment. But Hosea had received the promise of a wonderful reversal in future days. God would again say 'Ammi', 'My people', to his estranged children (1 : 9; 2 : 1, 23, *cf.* AV).

According to the Servant oracle, the Servant of the Lord, whom we have already seen as the leader of the new exodus, will speak to Zion the comforting word: 'You Ammi, you my people.' As the new exodus will be a radical deliverance, freedom from the bondage of corruption itself, and the resurrection of a dying world, the Servant may be proclaimed as the agent of God's new creation. 'I have put my words in your mouth, and I have covered you in the shadow of my hand, to plant heavens and to found earth and to say to Zion, "You Ammi, my people." '

The image of *planting* the heavens is strange indeed. There may have been a scribal error here; with a change of only one letter, it could read 'to stretch out' instead of 'to plant'. The old Syriac version read like this, and the RSV follows it. However, it is probably wiser to keep the traditional, more surprising, text. One might think of the skies as a tent to be planted. One can even retain the agricultural connotations of planting; the same image is prominent in the later prophecies of Isaiah and it is not absent from the Servant Songs. As God graciously plants and waters, salvation will 'germinate' or sprout (*cf.* 44 : 4; 45 : 8; 60 : 21; 61 : 3, 11). Of the 'new things' associated with the Servant's ministry, the Lord says, 'Before they spring forth (or sprout) I tell you of them' (42 : 9). Is there a relationship between the planting of the heavens, the sprouting of the new things, and the Servant as a young plant growing up out of dry ground (53 : 2)? Whatever the image of planting refers to, the entire Bible testifies to the fact that the new creation is not a mere bombastic display of power. It is a mysterious development of life, with small, easily despised beginnings. In other words, God's representative on earth and co-creator with him is none other than the suffering Servant.

Once the Servant's role and dignity have been recognized, we are not too surprised to hear typical Servant language used in the Lord's 'I-discourse'. In 51:4, 5 God proclaims:

> A law (*tôrâ*) will go forth from me,
>> and my justice (*mišpat*) for a light to the peoples. . . .
> The coastlands wait for me.

The Lord claims as his own the mission that the first Song defined as the Servant's. How strong a hint of the unity between them!

My conclusion may shock some readers, but I can draw no other: in these passages we are not far from the highest New Testament christology, such as that found in the fourth Gospel. The Servant does nothing of himself; the Lord always stands with him and will gloriously vindicate him. He is the Word made flesh, the principle and mediator of a new creation and of a new people of God, for in the beginning he was the mediator through whom all things were made. He is Jesus, whose vindication brings a crisis upon the world; Jesus, before whom every man makes his decision for eternity.

The fourth Song: Behold, the Lamb of God!

Behold, my servant shall prosper,
he shall be exalted and lifted up,
and shall be very high.
14 *As many were astonished at him—*
his appearance was so marred, beyond human semblance,
and his form beyond that of the sons of men—
15 *so shall he startle many nations;*
kings shall shut their mouths because of him;
for that which has not been told them they shall see,
and that which they have not heard they shall understand.

53:1 *Who has believed what we have heard?*
And to whom has the arm of the Lord been revealed?
2 *For he grew up before him like a young plant,*
and like a root out of dry ground;
he had no form or comeliness that we should look at him,
and no beauty that we should desire him.
3 *He was despised and rejected by men;*
a man of sorrows, and acquainted with grief;
and as one from whom men hide their faces
he was despised, and we esteemed him not.

4 *Surely he has borne our griefs*
and carried our sorrows;
yet we esteemed him stricken,
smitten by God, and afflicted.
5 *But he was wounded for our transgressions,*
he was bruised for our iniquities;
upon him was the chastisement that made us whole,
and with his stripes we are healed.

⁶ *All we like sheep have gone astray;*
   we have turned every one to his own way;
and the Lord has laid on him
   the iniquity of us all.

⁷ *He was oppressed, and he was afflicted,*
   yet he opened not his mouth;
like a lamb that is led to the slaughter,
   and like a sheep that before its shearers is dumb,
   so he opened not his mouth.
⁸ *By oppression and judgment he was taken away;*
   and as for his generation, who considered
that he was cut off out of the land of the living,
   stricken for the transgression of my people?
⁹ *And they made his grave with the wicked*
   and with a rich man in his death,
although he had done no violence,
   and there was no deceit in his mouth.

¹⁰ *Yet it was the will of the Lord to bruise him;*
   he has put him to grief;
when he makes himself an offering for sin,
   he shall see his offspring, he shall prolong his days;
the will of the Lord shall prosper in his hand;
¹¹   *he shall see the fruit of the travail of his soul and be satisfied;*
by his knowledge shall the righteous one, my servant,
   make many to be accounted righteous;
   and he shall bear their iniquities.
¹² *Therefore I will divide him a portion with the great,*
   and he shall divide the spoil with the strong;
because he poured out his soul to death,
   and was numbered with the transgressors;
yet he bore the sin of many,
   and made intercession for the transgressors (Is. 52:13—53:12).

If ever a prophecy deserved to be called 'gospel', 'good news',
it is the fourth Servant Song. Franz Delitzsch aptly commented
that this, the 'great' Servant Song, sounds as if it had been
written under the very cross of Golgotha.

Christian believers feel their hearts strangely warmed as they read this Song and recognize in it an incredibly precise picture of their Master. Both his career and his character they find delineated here with unrivalled clarity. Just as it is in the Song, so it was with him. The Servant 'grew up . . . like a root out of dry ground'; Jesus was born in obscurity and poverty. The Servant 'had no form or comeliness that we should look at him'; Jesus did not use ordinary human means to draw people to himself. The Servant was disbelieved, 'despised and rejected by men'; Jesus constantly met with unbelief and rejection. The Servant was 'a man of sorrows, and acquainted with grief'; Jesus, more than any man, knew the depths of suffering. The Servant 'had done no violence, and there was no deceit in his mouth'; none was able to convict Jesus of sin. Even so, just as the Servant was taken away 'by oppression and judgment', so Jesus was the victim of a miscarriage of justice. Yet the Servant 'opened not his mouth'; Jesus yielded himself, uncomplaining, to unjust punishment. The Servant was put to death, 'cut off out of the land of the living', and buried with the wicked; all this happened to Jesus. In his death the Servant was 'numbered with the transgressors', Jesus was crucified—a criminal's death—with two thieves. The righteous Servant shall 'make many to be accounted righteous'; Jesus died, the just for the unjust, to justify us by his blood. The Servant rose again to 'prolong his days'; who but the Lord Jesus has ever risen from the dead, never to die again, and has been supremely exalted? Some have even noted that just as Jesus rose, ascended and was glorified, so there are three corresponding verbs in 52:13—the Servant 'shall be exalted and lifted up, and shall be very high'. The risen Servant vanquishes his enemies, bringing God's plan to completion; the risen, glorified Jesus, who died with the cry 'It is finished' on his lips, has been highly exalted so that every knee should bow at his name.

Not only are the facts of the New Testament revealed here, but the meaning of those facts as well. Christians often quote from Isaiah 53 in order to point to the central truth of the doctrine of the atonement: that Christ atoned by penal substitution. No less than ten times is this thought forcefully expressed in the chapter (verses 4–6, 8, 11, 12). Jesus was punished not for any wrong he had done, but on behalf of the guilty, in their stead. He 'bore' their sins—a conventional Old Testament phrase for the infliction of punishment.

As children, some of us were taught to make a personal paraphrase of the whole passage; to read it aloud, replacing 'we', 'us', 'ours', with 'I', 'me', 'my' or with our own name. Instead of 'he', 'the servant', we were taught to say 'Jesus'. This childlike blending of interpretation and application embodies a Christian's spontaneous attitude to the Song. God forbid that we should blush if we too are contented with such a simplicity.

The spirit of our age has made us grow shy of supernatural prediction. We feel it quite inappropriate to speak of this kind of miracle. But what right have we to hide what God saw fit to reveal? Who are we to despise the signs of the Lord's wisdom? Blaise Pascal was bold enough to write, 'Prophecies are the greatest proof of Jesus Christ.' Isaiah's prophecies are surely the most convincing of them all. The fulfilment of prophecy is one of the main arguments of the prophet's own apologetic. Just before the first Servant Song, it is emphasized that the one true God authenticates himself through the fulfilment of his words, something that false gods cannot do (41:21-24). When events that have been foretold come to pass, the Lord establishes his sovereign position both above and within history. By the fulfilment of God's words, too, the foundation for faith is laid. Faith is the gift of God, the fruit of his Spirit, the effect of his word; and also a responsible decision taken when we honestly come to terms with reality. In our day, when God is constantly explained away as a product of wishful thinking, a creation of human fear and desire; when faith is misunderstood as an escapist device or as a leap in the dark, the correspondence of words and facts, of Isaiah's prophecy and Jesus' life, should stimulate a true, biblical faith in us.

We believe not only that Jesus is the Servant (that is, that Jesus fulfils what is written of the Servant—a *retrospective* interpretation of the prophecy), but also that the Servant is Jesus, and him crucified (that is to say that Isaiah, from his own vantage point in history, looked forward to the coming of Jesus and actually *spoke about him*). We dare read, '*Jesus* was wounded for *my* transgressions, *Jesus* was bruised for *my* iniquities'—

indeed, this is the most adequate interpretation of the evidence deduced from a truly scientific study of the Song.

Our aim, however, has been to interpret these Servant prophecies first of all within their original, historical context. What did they mean for the prophet and his disciples, and for those who first heard them? We shall follow this method in our study of the last Song also. This means not renouncing the New Testament truth of the passage but finding that truth afresh in its Old Testament setting.

Textual problems

When we turn to the text, we find that a brief comparison of several biblical versions brings disconcerting differences to light. It may be that this part of the text has suffered more than the rest at the hands of early scribes. Occasionally, we may be justified in preferring readings found not in the traditional rabbinic (Massoretic) text, but in ancient versions or other manuscripts. With the great majority of modern scholars, for instance, we would restore one letter at the end of 53:8 and read, 'He was . . . stricken *to death* for the transgression of my people.' in 53:11, the great Isaiah scroll from Qumran has confirmed the Greek version which reads, 'He shall *see light after* the travail of his soul.' Yet we believe that many of the complexities and obscurities of the passage were there from the beginning; they reflect the prophet's amazement at the things the Spirit of God moved him to say. He just cannot find words, it seems, to express himself accurately. So we should not suspect that a copyist's error underlies every strangeness that perplexes us. Many modern versions lack proper caution in their tendency to 'correct' the Received Text of the Song: the RSV is sometimes guilty on this score, as we shall see.

Poetic structure

The fact that there are enigmatic expressions in the Song (mostly in 52:14, 15; 53:8–10) is certainly no sign of careless writing. Once the structure of the Song is recognized, it is easy to discern in it the well-organized work of a master builder. The most obvious feature is the repetition of the opening theme —supreme success, total victory—in the closing verse; a literary

device known as *inclusio*. Equally striking is the strophic
arrangement: five stanzas of regularly increasing length. This
feature can be seen clearly in the RSV, which sets out each
stanza separately. Furthermore, the great evangelical scholar
E. J. Young has shown that the first stanza functions as a kind
of prologue, summarizing the main themes of the prophecy. In
the four remaining stanzas, we find an interesting symmetry:
the second and fourth state facts, while the third and fifth
present the meaning of those facts. There are, then, two pairs
of stanzas, and in each pair the emphasis is first on fact, and
then on the significance of the facts.

Translation problems

By recognizing the prologue status of the first stanza, two
quite important translation problems can be solved. In both
cases our view, following E. J. Young and other evangelical
scholars, is that the traditional rendering (as found in the old
Latin Vulgate and the AV) should be retained.

The first problem concerns the meaning of the first verb in
52:15, of which the traditional rendering is 'sprinkle', and
which the RSV translates as 'startle'. The Hebrew verb appears
several times in the Old Testament, and it always means 'to
sprinkle'. It indicates the priests' liturgical action in the ritual
of sacrifice and purification (*cf.* Lv. 4:6; 8:11; 14:7). Now, if
the first stanza of the Song is taken as a summary of what
follows, then somewhere, further down the Song, there should
be an explanation of this verb. The fifth stanza helps us here. It
defines at greater length the sacrificial nature and expiatory
value of the Servant's sufferings. Many modern scholars,
however, think that 'sprinkle' seems not to fit the context. They
prefer to follow the Greek version (the Septuagint) and translate, with the RSV, 'So shall he startle many nations.' In this
translation, there is no thought of atonement present.

The burden of proof, then, surely rests with those who
would reject 'sprinkle'. Any other meaning has to be con-
structed in a purely hypothetical way; for instance, by saying
that 'to sprinkle' is also 'to splash', and that being splashed is
an image for the nations' sudden surprise. Granted, the syntax
at this point seems incoherent. It is as though the prophet

himself were stammering in amazement at the unspeakable darkness into which the Servant is to be plunged. Verses 14 and 15 may sound disconnected, but the train of thought is intelligible when the 'sprinkling' prophecy is seen to anticipate 53 : 10f. The Servant's death will be a sin offering; through the sprinkling of his blood many sinners will receive cleansing (*cf.* I Pet. 1 : 2).

The second problem is that of the relationship of the end of 52 : 15 to the first verse of chapter 53. 'That which they have not heard they shall understand. Who has believed what we have heard?' Many modern scholars put the rhetorical question of 53 : 1, and the verses that follow, into the mouths of the heathen kings of 52 : 15. But the prologue theory means that there is a break between the statement and the question, between the introduction and the main body of the poem; between the end of one stanza and the beginning of another. To say that 53 : 1 ff. is direct speech obscures both the message and the structure of the Song, and we would offer four exegetical reasons why this interpretation is to be rejected.

First, the literal translation of 53 : 1 is 'Who has believed our report (or, message)?' 'Our report' could possibly mean 'the report that was made to us', as the 'kings hypothesis' implies, but the use of the word elsewhere in the Old Testament suggests that the more natural interpretation is 'the message we—the prophets—are bringing'. The word is usually used of prophetic preaching (*cf.* 28 : 9; Je. 49 : 14; Ob. 1).

Second, the familiar feature of Hebrew poetry known as parallelism comes to our aid. The Old Testament poets would write in couplets, the second line almost repeating the sense of the first (synonymous parallelism), or completing it (synthetic parallelism), or stating its opposite (antithetic parallelism).[1] In

---

[1] Ps. 51 : 2 is a good example of synonymous parallelism:

> Wash me thoroughly from my iniquity,
> and cleanse me from my sin!

An example of synthetic parallelism is Ps. 119 : 77—

> Let thy mercy come to me, that I may live,
> for thy law is my delight.

—and of antithetic parallelism, Pr. 11 : 1—

> A false balance is an abomination to the Lord,
> but a just weight is his delight.

53:1 we have a clear case of synonymous parallelism: believing the report is equivalent to receiving the revelation of the 'arm' (the powerful deeds) of the Lord. This definitely supports our equation of 'our report' with the prophets' message.

Third, 53:1 is not, like the closing verses of chapter 52, concerned with the idea of amazement. The NEB paraphrase, 'Who would have believed what we have heard?' is misleading. The point of the verse is that no-one has understood, that the revelation was not perceived, that the report met unbelief.

Fourth, the kings of 52:15 are nowhere said to have uttered a word. In fact, the 'kings shall shut their mouths because of him'. Ancient Hebrew writers lacked our simple device for indicating direct speech—inverted commas—and would use an introductory formula such as 'He opened his mouth and spoke, saying . . .'. We have no reason to suppose that 53:1 is direct speech on the part of the kings.

Our conclusions are confirmed by the Dead Sea scroll of Isaiah, which divides the text after 52:12 and again after 52:13, agreeing with our prologue structure. We also have a double New Testament confirmation: the verse is quoted twice (Jn. 12:38; Rom. 10:16); each time as a prophetic comment and lament on Israel's unbelief. There can be no doubt, then; the first stanza is a gripping preface to the description of the way of the Servant, to the revelation which will encounter such little faith among the people.

The four main stanzas

After such a tremendous opening, the quieter tone of *the second stanza* is both a deft artistic variation and a reminder that suffering is not always dramatic, voiced in shouts and cries. It repeats a theme which we found in the other Songs, and uses one of Isaiah's favourite images for God's future of grace: a tiny sprout growing from that desolate place where the tallest cedars of Lebanon were felled (*cf.* 4:2; 6:13; 10:33—11:1). The emphasis of the stanza is on dereliction: the Servant is 'a man of sorrows, and acquainted with grief'—literally, 'known by grief', as a man is known by a friend. He will first of all undergo the subtle, almost hidden, psychological pain of *contempt*. The need for acceptance, esteem, acknowledgment, is one of the basic hungers of human personality, especially of such a sensitive and open personality as the Servant's. How agonizing to be starved of them! The Servant will be utterly despised by men: the word translated 'men' occurs here in a rare form, suggesting would-be mighty men, self-assertive men, full of pride at their success and virility. How different the Servant will be!

The third stanza is dominated by an antithesis: the antithesis between what we thought to be the cause of the Servant's doom, and what was the real cause. Self-righteously, like Job's friends, we thought that such sufferings could be interpreted only as divine retribution for vile personal sins; surely the Servant was smitten by God. How could we be so blind and stupid? Blinder and more stupid than David condemning his own conduct as he listened to Nathan's parable (2 Sa. 12: 1–9). The torments the Servant endured were *ours*. *We* were the guilty ones, and his sufferings were the retribution for *our* vile personal sins. It was for our sake that he submitted himself to undeserved punishment, that we might be healed. While we were sitting in judgment on him, we were really condemning ourselves, rebellious and vagrant sheep that we were! And yet there is hope for us, hope and healing, precisely because the Servant has borne our chastisement!

The Servant was assigned not only a suffering life, but also a suffering death. This is the clear revelation of *the fourth stanza*. He will be led as a sheep to the slaughter. He will be put to death and buried. The forensic vocabulary suggests that the Servant will undergo a trial and will suffer violence at the hands of 'justice'. According to D. F. Payne, the formula in verse 8 might be some fixed legal idiom.[2] We would propose the following translation:

> After arrest and sentence he was taken away,
>   and who cared where he went?
> He was cut off out of the land of the living,
>   stricken to death for the transgression of my people.

That the Servant will be the victim of a miscarriage of

[2] D. F. Payne, 'The Servant of the Lord: Language and Interpretation', *Evangelical Quarterly*, XLIII, no. 3, 1971, p. 135.

justice is important. It means that we should dispel the view that the sufferings foretold in the preceding verses would be those of physical disease. This view rests upon alternative translations of certain words in the third, fourth and tenth verses,[3] and is held by some modern scholars. But, as George Adam Smith pointed out, Isaiah's sufferer 'would have been either a leper or a convict, but hardly both'. The teaching in verses 5 and 6 bears out the relevance of the categories of condemnation and punishment.

A miscarriage of justice—and yet the fulfilment of God's plan! 'It was the will of the Lord to grind him': this is the literal translation of the opening of *the fifth stanza*. This statement proclaims how the Lord's design will be fully realized. The Servant's death will be a sin offering. It will involve the glorious vindication of the Servant, whose fruitful life beyond the grave will prove him to be the Righteous One. It centres in the justification or acquittal of those many transgressors among whom the Servant will be numbered, and for whom this whole intervention is to take place.

Two specific points here call for comment. First, while the fact that successful activity follows juridical execution implies resurrection—how could anyone miss it?—some have been disturbed by the absence of a clear statement that the Servant will rise again. Some scholars have tried to account for this by positing the influence of the Tammuz liturgy. Tammuz was an ancient Sumerian vegetation deity who descended to the underworld and returned annually, typifying the annual cycle of death and new growth in the vegetable world. This 'revivification' was assumed, but never described. This explanation, however, has now been generally discarded; apart from the fact that it is improbable that a prophet who denounces heathen worship should borrow ideas from idolatry in this way, the theory involves a dubious interpretation of ancient Near Eastern mythology. Tammuz' cyclic return from the underworld cannot really be called a revivification, much less a resurrection, and it cannot be compared with the Servant's unique exaltation. Without claiming to know all the prophet's reasons for writing as he did, we may observe that his interest lies in *the contrast of the two states*—shameful death and victorious

[3] See RSV margin, *ad loc.*

splendour—and not in the method of passage from the one to the other.

The second point relates to the beginning of 53:12. Most versions, like the RSV, render it: 'Therefore I will divide him a portion with the great, and he shall divide the spoil with the strong.' Who are these great and strong ones among whom the Servant is found? Actually, this question does not arise; it stems from an unfortunate translation. The first of these two words, translated 'great' (the only place where it is so translated in the RSV), is one which keeps recurring throughout the fourth Song; the scholar Joachim Jeremias has rightly labelled it a key word. In all other instances, including those immediately before and after this occurrence, it is rendered 'many'. Many were astonished at the Servant; he will sprinkle many nations; he will make many to be accounted righteous; he bore the sin of many. Such repetition is surely not without significance; consistency demands that the word be translated 'many' throughout the entire passage, and therefore also in verse 12: 'I will divide him a portion with the many.' The 'many' are the multitude of those who will benefit from the Servant's work.

This whole couplet is another case of synonymous parallelism.[4] Does the parallel word have to be translated 'strong'? By no means! Although this is its usual meaning, the second word may also be translated 'numerous'. Together, the words are often used as a pair in the Old Testament to denote multitude rather than might (*cf.* Ex. 1:7; Pr. 7:26; Zc. 8:22). The concluding promise of the Song, therefore, is not that the Servant will be promoted to the ranks of great captains and mighty warriors. The promise is that he will share the riches he has obtained by his victory with a multitude of needy men, for whom he freely consented to die.

A mystery of suffering

Even this cursory viewing of the Song's contents and development makes its central theme clear. The Servant's *suffering*, the depth and intensity of this suffering, the causes and meaning of this suffering, are the revealed mystery which the previous Songs had only gradually suggested. Rejection and trial have

[4] See above, p. 62.

been increasingly associated with the Servant's mission. In the first Song there was only a slight hint; we read there that the Servant would not faint or be crushed while fulfilling his calling (42:4), and we could deduce that he would meet adverse circumstances. In the second Song it became clearer; there the Servant tells us that for a time, at least, his work would seem to have failed: 'I have laboured in vain, I have spent my strength for nothing and vanity.' He will be called 'one deeply despised, abhorred by the nation' (49:4, 7). In the third Song, we saw the Servant insulted, tortured, falsely accused (50:6, 8 f.). But now the picture is complete, over-whelmingly complete. The Servant will be disfigured and condemned, interned as a criminal and put to death. As we have watched this suffering build up, we have seen the Servant pass from meekness to patience, from patience to flint-like courage, from courage to total obedience.

The chief question now is this: what elements in the pro-phet's mind did the Spirit of God use in giving this revelation? He does not operate in a vacuum. How did the Spirit lead Isaiah towards the vision of the Servant's suffering? To what previously known truths could Isaiah's disciples link the strange, newly revealed truth, and begin to understand it?

In none of the other Songs is the inadequacy of the 'collec-tive' interpretations so glaring as in the fourth Servant Song. Even some scholars who maintain that in the earlier Songs the Servant is Israel (either the whole nation or the remnant) grant that in this Song an individual must be in view. No prophecy attributes even a relative innocence to Israel or to the remnant. Isaiah certainly does not do so. Much less do the prophets attribute sinlessness to the nation! Isaiah says that the Servant will die 'for the transgression of my people'; the prophet includes himself among the many whose sins the Servant will bear. The Servant, therefore, is not Israel.

Not a few Psalms voice laments about sufferings inflicted by evildoers on the (relatively) innocent (see Pss. 7, 17, 18). Did Isaiah get his clue from these Psalms? Was the Servant, for him, primarily the typical righteous, godly man, and there-fore only secondarily the man of sorrows? Is the key to be found in the principle that all who live godly lives will suffer persecu-tion? We acknowledge a measure of truth in this thought. Yet it is not specific enough. The connection between righteousness and suffering is not tight enough in the Old Testament. The main theme of the fourth Song is not that the Servant was blameless (though he was), but that he willingly died for us, thus fulfilling the Lord's mysterious decree. Who then was the Servant? What figures in his contemporary culture did Isaiah use as models in painting his portrait of the Servant?

The prophet figure

The first three Servant Songs have pictured the Servant not only as a godly man, but as a man with a mission—essentially a prophetic mission. Could it be that in Isaiah's mind, suffering and the prophetic ministry were closely associated? True, not all prophets were ill-received in Israel; Nathan, for example, enjoyed a favoured position in David's court, and Isaiah himself was influential under Hezekiah's reign. But on the whole, the prophets were God's most abused and maltreated servants. They were sent, primarily, 'to declare to Jacob his transgression and to Israel his sin' (Mi. 3:8). How could they possibly have failed to meet opposition? The bitterest attacks, of course, came from the rich and the mighty. These the prophets rebuked with relentless vigour. The indomitable Elijah had to flee for his life from Queen Jezebel. Talmudic tradition tells us that Isaiah himself died a martyr's death, being sawn in two when Hezekiah's godless son, Manasseh, reinstated idolatry (*cf.* Heb. 11:37). Jerusalem has indeed been guilty of killing the prophets and stoning those who are sent to her (Mt. 23:37). In fact, stoning was the death reserved by his exiled compatriots for Jeremiah in Egypt. Jeremiah! The Old Testament 'man of sorrows'! Most commentators have been struck by the great similarity between the cup Jeremiah had to drink and the fate of the Servant in the fifty-third chapter of Isaiah. Jeremiah applies to himself the very same image as the one used of the Servant; that of the lamb being led to the slaughter (Je. 11:19; *cf.* Is. 53:7).

It is not a very difficult step from the thought that the Servant will be '*the* Prophet' to the thought that he will plumb the depths of rejection and persecution. That may well have been part of Isaiah's logic. According to the earlier Songs, as we have seen, the Servant is not only to be *the* Prophet, but the 'Prophet like Moses'. Moses' life was a hard one. The stiffnecked nation of Israel constantly rebelled against his leadership. The sacred record goes so far as to state that Moses even bore God's wrath because of the sins of the people, while he is frequently pictured as the great intercessor for the guilty (Dt. 3:26; 4:21; 9:18; Ps. 106:23).

Not only are the similarities striking, however; the contrasts are too. The Servant's *sinlessness* places him apart from the whole company of the Old Testament prophets, including Moses. Isaiah himself had been initiated into the prophetic office through conviction of sin. 'Woe is me!' he had cried, 'For I am lost; for I am a man of unclean lips, and I dwell in the midst of a people of unclean lips' (6:5). He had confessed a full share in the common filth.

In answer to Jeremiah's tearful prayers, God both encourages and reprehends him. Words of comfort are intertwined with words of rebuke (*e.g.* Je. 15:19).

For all his model meekness, Moses stumbled. The book of Numbers makes no attempt to cover his faults. In chapter 20, for instance, his unbelief and disobedience are recorded frankly: the Lord had given him clear instructions for miraculously providing the thirsty wilderness wanderers with water; but Moses, instead of obeying God in faith, just lost his temper. But on the Servant's lips no violent words were ever found. Moses was provoked, and 'spoke words that were rash'; but the Servant, though 'he was oppressed and . . . afflicted, . . . opened not his mouth' (Ps. 106:33; Is. 53:7).

In addition to this contrast, there is another which seems to show that the interpretation of the Servant's suffering simply as prophetic suffering—even as the supreme example of that suffering—is inadequate. Both the meaning and the result of the Servant's suffering were radically different. However inevitable the suffering might have been for a true prophet, it was not an integral part of his mission; he was not sent specifically to suffer. Suffering, for the prophets, came into the category of 'occupational hazard'. Not so for the Servant: 'it was the will of the Lord to grind him' (53:10). The last Song, the culmination of the revelation concerning him, does not mention his teaching ministry like the earlier Songs; it tells us that he came specifically *to suffer* and to give his life for many. The prophets, like Moses, often had to bear the consequences of the sins of others; the Servant will bear the sins themselves. His passion will be an act for others, a work through which sinners will find healing and righteousness before God. This is without parallel in the lives of the prophets.

Though it never materialized, the *idea* of a prophet bearing the sins of others did emerge once. This fact deserves more notice than it has received. The idea occurs in Moses' dealings with God (see Ex. 32). While Moses was communing with God on mount Sinai, the people treacherously made an idol, a golden calf, and devoted a whole day to its orgiastic worship. Moses, on his descent, was furiously angry and immediately put a ruthless purge under way. Notice what Moses says to the people on the next day. 'You have sinned a great sin. And now I will go up to the Lord; perhaps I can make atonement for your sin' (verse 30). What kind of atoning action does Moses have in view? As he prays to the Lord, he makes an astounding proposal: 'If thou wilt forgive their sin—and if not, blot me, I pray thee, out of thy book' (verse 32). Moses was saying not 'Destroy me with them'—a word of despair—but 'Destroy me *instead of* them.' This is clear from the Lord's answer: 'Whoever has sinned against me, *him* will I blot out of my book' (verse 33). Moses had thought he could yield up his own life in atonement for the sins of Israel! This idea is surely relevant to our understanding of Isaiah 53. The concept contained in that chapter was not entirely new. But equally significant is the fact that the Lord's reply to Moses was 'No—it cannot be. It is not your mission, and it is not the right time.' How was Isaiah led to discern that what was impossible for Moses and the prophets was to be the Servant's own appointed mission?

The king figure

Just as the function of the Servant's suffering was different from that of the prophets' suffering, so is the outcome different as well. Never is the suffering of the prophets rewarded with an exaltation like the Servant's. Suffering is not the only theme of the fourth Song. There are also promises of prosperity (the first verb in 52:13 means 'succeed through wisdom'), the dazzling of heathen kings, the division of the spoil. What have these to do with suffering and an ignominious death? How did all these ideas become linked together in the minds of Isaiah and his disciples? Does the promise of exaltation throw any light on the meaning of the Servant's suffering?

A quick look at what the Song says about the Servant's exaltation is enough to enable us to perceive its nature. The triumph awaiting the Servant is indeed *royal*. The Servant is King! The fact that 'the will of the Lord shall prosper in his hand' bears this out. In Israel, the king was viceregent under God, and it was his task to carry out God's will and to lead the nation in the fulfilment of the divine plan. Moreover, we have already examined the 'sprout' image—'he grew up before him like a young plant, and like a root out of dry ground'—and we have seen that this image was used of the great King of the line of David, who was to come.[5] But if the Servant is a king, where does his suffering come in? We find it strange to link kingship with hardship.

We can obtain help on this point from an interesting source. The early scribes gave headings or titles to many of the Psalms. These titles embody ancient tradition. Many of the Psalms, such as Psalms 22 and 69, headed 'A Psalm of David', are in fact prayers in times of persecution. The Hebrew preposition translated 'of' does not necessarily mean 'written by', but can mean 'to' or 'referring to'. The preposition bears the third of these meanings in the titles of Canaanite psalms discovered at Ras Shamra. If we take Psalms 22 and 69 as being 'Psalms referring to David', the Messianic (kingly) interpretation given to them in the New Testament is born out: the trials depicted in them are not those of an anonymous individual but of the king himself; and the anointed king is the 'type' or foreshadower of the Messiah, the Anointed One.[6] Psalm 18, an undisputed 'royal psalm', powerfully depicts 'the chords of death' and 'the torrents of perdition' (verse 4). Its title describes it as 'A Psalm of David the servant of the Lord'. This phrase, 'the servant of

---

[5] See above, p. 17; *cf.* Is. 11:1 ff.

[6] Quotations from Ps. 22 are applied to or used by Jesus in Jn. 19:24 and Heb. 2:12. Quotations from Ps. 69 are similarly used in Jn. 2:17; 15:25 and Rom. 15:3. Both Psalms are echoed in the crucifixion narratives in Mt. 27, Mk. 15, Lk. 23 and Jn. 19.

the Lord', is mostly used elsewhere for Moses; is it a coincidence that it is used here of David? At any rate, as the kingly Servant will suffer, so David suffered, and so will the promised King-Messiah whom David foreshadowed.

How should we account for the idea of the suffering King? We can point to the *military obligations* of kingship: the king had to lead his people in battle, which often meant risking his life. Upon him the hatred of the nations was concentrated. They were not only the enemies of the king, but the enemies of the Lord as well. This meant that Israel's king was waging not merely a national war, but the battles of the Lord. It was his task to face not only human enemies, but the forces of evil which rose up to try to overthrow the Lord's people and plan.

Tribulation and triumph are also combined in the concept of God's *election* of the king. It was the king's destiny to be the Lord's lieutenant, his representative on earth, his 'chosen man' in a special sense. This was not only for the king's own sake, but also, and chiefly, for the sake of his people. He could be considered as the mirror of God's dealings with men. In him can be seen both the weakness and vulnerability of man, and the riches of electing grace.

Both these themes—the king as the Lord's fighter, and as the man elect for the sake of his people—appear in the fourth Servant Song. In the darkness of the Servant's death there is a triumphant encounter with the powers of evil: the Lord gives the Servant the victory, and he shares its benefits with the many.

The sacrifice figure

Not even a synthesis of prophetic and royal suffering is an adequate solution of our problem. The king may die *for the sake* of his people, but he does not lay down his life *instead* of them. He will judge transgressors and mete out their punishments; it is not his calling to be numbered among them or to bear what they deserved in order that they may be accounted righteous! Where did Isaiah find the principle of substitution? He tells us himself. He found it in the *sin offering*. The reference in 53:10 to a technical term used in the context of the sacrificial system is unmistakable. The book of Leviticus rules that if sinful man, under the holy wrath of a holy God, would approach the Lord, he must sacrifice a spotless victim in his place (see Lv. 4 and 5). This is how atonement is made. This is the core of the institution of sacrifice. The Servant 'makes *himself* an offering for sin'; he offers not another life, but his own, as a sin offering. Since he offers the sacrifice, he is the priest; since he offers himself, he is the sacrifice. He himself is the Lamb of God.

Here at last is the key! We cannot explain the statements and vocabulary of the fourth Song unless we grant that the author perceived, however dimly, the fact that the Levitical system was a type or foreshadowing of what was to come. Isaiah must have understood that the various sin and trespass offerings were a prefiguration of a final, perfect atonement, in which the substitute would not be a mere symbol as in the animal sacrifices. To Isaiah it was revealed that the promised Prophet would not only suffer, like most prophets, but that the decisive act of his ministry would be to offer himself as the great and final sacrificial victim.

Once we understand this, the whole passage becomes clear. Now we understand the statement in the prologue, that the Servant will 'sprinkle' many nations, just as the Levitical priests sprinkled the blood of the sacrifices in the rite of purification. Above all, we understand why the Servant's suffering is central; he will be born specifically to die, to offer himself as a sacrificial victim slain for the sins of his people, thus fulfilling also the priestly mission of making atonement. Having realized this, we can see how all the benefits which the Servant wins for his people fit together. All of them proceed from the Servant's work of *atonement.* We were guilty and condemned, under the wrath of a God who cannot look upon iniquity, but we have peace with God because the Servant has borne our sins and paid our penalty, removing from us the cause of God's wrath. We were riddled with the disease of sin; there was nothing in us 'but bruises and sores and bleeding wounds' (Is. 1:6): but we receive healing because the Servant has borne in his own body the hideous deserts of our sin. For us he was wounded and bruised and his flesh was lacerated. We had no righteousness of our own, no defence before God's judgment throne, but the Servant has made us to be accounted righteous;

in knowing him we are acquitted and accepted at God's tribunal. Now we can see how gloriously the new Moses will transcend the old. The prophet of Sinai could only impose God's law on us; he could never fulfil it for us.

The new exodus of which Isaiah has already spoken will indeed be accomplished with the blood of a better paschal lamb. The passover sacrifice, though not a sin or trespass offering, was substitutionary like them. A shadow of what was to come, the first passover sacrifice marked a redemption, and was the means by which God's wrath was averted.

The old exodus heralded the old covenant given through Moses: the new exodus heralds the introduction of the new covenant. We have already met the covenant theme in the Songs.[7] This new covenant will be sealed with the Servant's blood—blood which, unlike that of bulls and goats and sheep, is able to wash away all sin for ever. The unprecedented magnitude, efficacy and finality of the Servant's work proclaim him the agent of that new creation of which Isaiah has already sung. Prophet, king, priest, sacrifice, deliverer, mediator of a new covenant, agent of a new creation—this is the Servant. How much more than a servant!

The many

Now that we have seen the Servant as the one who fulfils all these roles, we are better able to understand his relationship to those to whom his passion and death bring blessing. The earlier Songs have given us clues about the people who will enjoy what the Servant will provide. There are several promises in the Book of Consolation of the grace and splendour which are to be conferred on Zion (see, *e.g.*, 49:19–23; 51:21—52:2, 54:1–3). But in the fourth Song, the description is complete.

Who are these people for whom the Servant will suffer? We can give three answers to this question. First, a clue is found in the Servant's work. As priest he will represent the *guilty* nation; as victim he will be offered in the place of the *sinner*. Those for whom he will die are beset by grief and sorrows, burdened by transgressions and iniquities; sick, wilful and perverse. Not only this: they have rejected and despised him

[7] See above, pp. 30, 40f.

through whose work they are to find peace, forgiveness and healing (53:4-6).

Second, the Song gives them a twofold name. They are 'the many', including those from 'many nations'; and they are Israel. Is this a contradiction? Many nations, one nation? It agrees with the second Song, which pictures the Servant both as the head of the true Israel and as a light to the Gentiles. The members of the Qumran community on the shores of the Dead Sea in the period between the Testaments regarded themselves as the true Israel. They used 'the many' as a regular, official title. But they only half understood what Isaiah was trying to say, for they forgot that 'the many' was to include Gentiles. When Jesus later used the same word to designate the beneficiaries of his sacrifice, speaking of himself as 'a ransom for many' (Mt. 20:28 and parallels), he freed the term from national exclusivism. In the New Testament there is revealed the mystery which abolishes the apparent contradiction: as the covenant is new, so the true Israel is a new Israel. Men and women of many nations may, as Paul puts it, be grafted into the old olive tree and made members of God's own people (Rom. 11:13-24). The international or supranational character of the Servant's Israel perfectly fits what had been foretold of the kingdom of the Messiah; that it would reach to the uttermost parts of the earth (Pss. 2, 72; Am. 9:12, explained in Acts 15:15ff.). This agreement is a further confirmation of the Servant's royal Messiahship.

But how do you join the many? How can a person become a member of the multitude of the Servant's community? Our third description suggests an answer. The Servant is to see his *offspring*, the fruit of his work (53:10). Since the Servant has been portrayed as a prophetic teacher, the word is best understood as referring to his spiritual children, his disciples. This means that no-one is healed or forgiven as an *automatic* result of the work of atonement regardless of one's inward disposition. On the contrary, there must be a subjective as well as an objective relationship with the Servant—a relationship of personal love, trust and obedience. This requirement is not absent from the sacrificial law itself, since that law rules that no atonement is possible for the man who sins 'with a high hand' (deliberately, blatantly), and who refuses to listen to the priest (Nu. 15:30,

31; Dt. 17:12). The same thought is expressed in the fourth
Song, which states that it is 'by his knowledge', or through
knowing the Servant, that the many will be justified (53:11).
These words seem to point to a personal relationship between
the Servant and those who will benefit from his work. Sins will
not be forgiven automatically. Only if the individual is united
to the Servant as a personal disciple will he be accounted
righteous.

Synthesis and fulfilment

Christian hearts are burning. Such a doctrine of justification, a
prophetic, royal and priestly Servant of the Lord—do we not
have here the beginning of the synthesis of the various strands
of Israel's hope; a synthesis fulfilled in Christ? It cannot be
denied that the three cardinal offices which are called 'Christic'
—those of prophet, priest and king—are here brought together.
Among the heathen nations, the offices of king and priest were
not separated. By contrast, in Israel the offices were strictly
demarcated. King Uzziah had to learn this the hard way:
when he tried to burn incense on the altar, a rite which only
the priests were allowed to perform, the consequences were
bitter (2 Ch. 26:16ff.). This strict separation was a sign
of the incompleteness of the old dispensation, of its 'not yet'
character.

But the union of both offices had been foretold. David's
oracle in Psalm 110 pointed forward to the union of priest and
king in fulfilment of the Messianic hope. The Messiah would be
a priest after the order of Melchizedek, who was king of
Salem as well as priest of God Most High. Isaiah goes far
beyond this idea as he shows that the new priesthood will
involve a new sacrifice—the Priest's self-sacrifice (*cf.* Heb.
7:27)—and as he links the whole priest-king scheme with the
promise of the new Moses.

We may observe that Zechariah, the Old Testament prophet most influenced by the Servant Songs, shows a great
interest in the relationship between the royal and priestly
offices. In chapter 4 he uses two olive trees to symbolize 'the
two anointed who stand by the Lord' (verse 14). One of these
is Zerubbabel, the prince, a descendant of David; the other

must be Joshua the high priest. Both king and high priest were instituted into the office by the rite of anointing. In Zechariah's vision, the two are closely associated. Later, the oracle of 6:9–14, with the high priest wearing two crowns (verse 11, RSV margin) when the coming of the future Messianic king is proclaimed, binds them even more tightly together; verse 13 emphasizes the thought of unity ('peaceful understanding') between kingship and priesthood.[8]

In the grand and decisive vision of chapter 3, Zechariah describes the synthesis with amazing economy of words. He proclaims that the Servant of the Lord is the same figure as the Branch, a well-known title for the Davidic Messiah since Jeremiah's time (Jer. 23:5). Yet, at the same time, he does not choose Zerubbabel, the Davidic prince, to stand as the type of the Messiah; he designates Joshua, the high priest, as the foreshadowing type of the Servant-Branch (3:8). Thus it is clear that the Servant will be not only the royal Messiah, but also a priest. He will fulfil both types, he will hold both offices. And the next verse carries further the thought of the Messiah as priest; Zechariah envisions a final day of atonement in which the Lord will wipe away the guilt of the land once and for all. In so small a compass, there could hardly be a more complete commentary on the last Servant Song. This is indeed the gospel before the Gospels.

Synthesis, of course, involves reinterpretation. The new priesthood and sacrifices are not mere reduplications of the old.[9] The new exodus delivers God's people from a different Babylon from that of Nebuchadnezzar—the Babylon of our own sin. The Servant's kingship, especially, will be different. This may be the reason why the royal aspect of the Servant is suggested rather than told. He rises on high as King of kings, but it is 'not by might, nor by power' (Zc. 4:6). His royal wisdom leads him to royal success, but by what a strange way! What is the spoil he shares with the many but righteousness, peace, and healing, because he bore the sins of the many? He

[8] See also Zc. 12:12 f. where the royal family of David, with the specific clan of Nathan his son, is mentioned together with the family of Levi, with the specific priestly clan of Shimei.

[9] The Letter to the Hebrews explains in detail the relationship between 'shadow' and 'reality' in the sacrificial system and its fulfilment.

is the Lion of the tribe of Judah, but he stands before God's throne as a Lamb that has been slain (Rev. 5:5, 6).

The many are to remember the way of the Servant as they share in his triumph. The New Testament reveals that they—we—are made in him kings, priests and prophets (see, *e.g.*, 1 Pet. 2:9). We do well to remember what kind of kingship this is—a kingship like his. We are to follow in his steps. This thought seems to be present in the book of Daniel. In Daniel 12:3 the Hebrew is strongly reminiscent of the language of the fourth Servant Song. 'Those who are wise shall shine like the brightness of the firmament; and those who turn many to righteousness, like the stars for ever and ever.' The word 'wise' is a form of the verb used in Isaiah 52:13, 'Behold, my servant shall succeed-through-wisdom.' The wise are not able to add to the Servant's work by which he makes many to be accounted righteous, but they will be instruments in the application of that work. In turning many to righteousness, they share in the Servant's ministry. Daniel makes it clear, too, that these wise ones will also go the way of suffering which the Servant trod. 'They shall fall by sword and flame, by captivity and plunder . . . to refine and to cleanse them and to make them white' (Dn. 11:33, 35).

Wisdom: this is the emphasis in Daniel's echoes of the Song, and it is a fitting note for us to strike in conclusion. The Servant's wisdom is the wisdom of God, a seeming foolishness which is wiser than the wisdom of men, and which cannot be understood by the unspiritual man (*cf.* 1 Cor. 1 and 2). It is wisdom indeed, and we are called to understand it. Only this way could God's victory over evil be radical and complete, as indeed it is. Evil could not be conquered in the way in which an inferior power is conquered by a superior, for then evil would not have been vanquished as evil. It is not a created power among others; it is, as Augustine saw, non-created, yet real, an unthinkable perversion of order, a scandalous corruption of goodness. Through the divine wisdom, evil was defeated, turned against itself in self-destruction. By death the Servant broke the power of death (Heb. 2:14). By concentrating upon himself all men's criminal hatred, by taking upon himself the most unjust and undeserved of sufferings, he offered the sacrifice which wipes away all sin for ever for all those who know him. And so the victory was total. O the wisdom of God! Worthy is the Son of God, Jesus Christ, who became the Servant—the Lamb—to be crowned Lord of all!

> Worthy art thou . . .
> for thou wast slain and by thy blood didst ransom men for God
> from every tribe and tongue and people and nation,
> and hast made of them a kingdom and priests to our God,
> and they shall reign on earth (Rev. 5:9, 10).